EASY TO MAKE

DOLLS

EASY TO MAKE
DOLLS

Audrey Vincente Dean
Series consultant: Eve Harlow

BROCKHAMPTON PRESS
LONDON

For Dick, with love

First published in Great Britain in 1992
by Anaya Publishers Ltd, Strode House,
44-50 Osnaburgh Street, London NW1 3ND

This edition published 1996 by Brockhampton Press,
a member of Hodder Headline PLC Group

Editor Eve Harlow
Design by Design 23
Photographer Di Lewis
Illustrator Kate Simunek
Artwork Stan North

British Library Cataloguing in Publication Data

Vincente Dean, Audrey
Easy to make dolls. – (Easy to make)
1. Dollmaking. Dollmaking
I. Title II. Series
745.592

ISBN 1-86019-144-4

Typeset by Design 23
Colour reproduction by Columbia Offset, Singapore
Printed and bound in EC

CONTENTS

Introduction   6

1: PLAY DOLLS
Two-faced dolls   10
Frog prince   16
Ballerina   24
Sweet Sue   28
Sock gnome   36
Happy clown   39
Cuddly rabbit   44

2: USEFUL DOLLS
Message Doll   50
Tidy Teddy   53
Doorstop cat   58
Victorian lady   63

3: LITTLE DOLLS
Christmas fairies   70
House of dolls   73
Dolly pocket   86
Baby bunting   88
Baby doll   92
Flying witch   94

4: BETTER DOLL MAKING   96

Acknowledgement   112

Introduction

Doll making is a craft for everyone. The basic techniques are simple and the finished results will bring hours of pleasure to children and adults alike.

For thousands of years, human figures have been reproduced as dolls. Mostly, dolls are playthings for children but they have also had a decorative and a ritual use.

Early dolls were often crudely made from rags or from wood or clay, sometimes wrapped in scraps of fabric. In later years, as materials and tools became more widely available and craftsmanship developed, dolls were more carefully constructed and their clothes reflected the fashions of the day.

Victorian dolls had heads of porcelain or wax with delicately painted features and, sometimes, wigs of real hair. These dolls were dressed in sumptuous velvets and silks, their garments trimmed with real lace, ribbons and, sometimes, semi-precious stones. The dolls were rarely played with by children and for this reason, many examples in fine condition exist today in museums and private collections. Fabric dolls were also made and those sewn by our great, great-grandmothers were probably similar to some of those in this book.

Because they were cheaper to produce they tended to get more wear from their owners and so there are few examples of rag dolls around that are more than 100 years old.

Making a doll yourself is very different from buying one for a gift. The child who receives the doll knows you have spent time on it, and that it is unique and therefore, the doll is treasured even more. Also, creating something with your own hands is a very enjoyable and satisfying experience.

Especially for beginners

There are many people who have wanted to try their hand at doll making but they have been put off because they think they lack the necessary sewing skills. When I prepared this book, I wanted to encourage beginners and so I have tried to keep the instructions simple and clear. The colour photographs will help you to succeed with the patterns so always study them carefully before starting a project. If there are some techniques which are strange to you or where you feel a little uncertain, then refer to the last chapter – everything you want to know is there.

You will see that the step-by-step instructions for each project are numbered. It is a good idea to read through the whole of each step before working it because it may contain several different operations. Reading it through will show you exactly what is to be achieved at this stage.

The dolls in this book fall into three categories. Play Dolls are especially for children and most will survive a lot of handling. Some dolls in this chapter are for make-believe games.

The chapter on Useful Dolls has designs with a specific purpose – such as the Tidy Teddy which hangs on the bedroom door or bedpost and stores nightclothes away neatly.

The Little Dolls chapter has all kinds of small dolls in it (such as the family who live in a carry house with their cat) and also has ideas for quick-to-make dolls. This chapter also has a fearsome witch on a broomstick – just the thing to make for a Hallowe'en decoration.

The Better Doll Making chapter at the end of the book is full of useful information on the craft of doll making. Here you will find what you need in the way of tools and equipment. Different kinds of suitable materials are discussed, together with ideas for obtaining special fabrics and trims. Pattern making is in this chapter and the know-how for enlarging and reducing patterns. Then the procedures for cutting out fabric and preparing to sew are covered with some special information on stuffing dolls properly so that your toys have a professional finish. The seams and the stitches you will be using to make dolls are in this special chapter together with ideas for working doll's features in different ways. Making hair styles for both girl and boy dolls is a fascinating aspect of the craft and I have worked out some simple and impressive techniques that you will enjoy trying. In this section, you will also find tips and hints on applying ribbons and lace, and making bows and tassels.

Safety first

Of all the dolls in this book, only the Cuddly rabbit in the Play Dolls chapter is suitable for very young children although the Two-faced dolls can be adapted into safe and attractive grab toys. Most of the dolls are carefully constructed, even those made from junk materials, and would not be suitable for a young child.

However, when you are making dolls for children of any age, it is always a good idea to use flame-retardant fabrics and trims whenever possible. Embroidered eyes will last longer – and be safer – than sewn-on buttons. Felt features are safe as long as they are securely sewn to the doll.

Something from nothing

Children rarely care about how much a doll has cost – we've all seen how a child will wrap a piece of wood in a jumper and cuddle it for a 'baby'. Colour, character – and humour – appeal to children far more and the dolls in this book have all of these qualities. Some designs are made from throw-away items – empty drinks cans, jars, bottles, cardboard tubes, discarded tights and stockings – so this book is not only a treasure house of fascinating projects, it also gives you, the reader, an opportunity to recycle items you would normally throw away. I hope that you will have as much fun making the dolls as I had in designing them.

ONE

Play Dolls

Two-faced dolls

On one side, the sleepy-head doll is dressed in night clothes, on the other side a wide-awake doll is dressed for play.
There are both boy and girl versions.

Materials for boy doll
Height 10in (25cm)
9¹/₂in (24cm) square of pink fabric
  for head
9¹/₂in (24cm) square of fabric for
  pyjamas
4 x 9¹/₂in (10 x 24cm) of fabric for shirt
5¹/₂ x 9¹/₂in (14 x 24cm) for trousers
Stranded embroidery threads
Five ¹/₄in (6mm) buttons
Jersey fabric or wool for hair
Polyester toy filling

Materials for girl doll
9¹/₂in (24cm) square of pink fabric for
  head
6 x 9in (15 x 24cm) of pink fabric for legs
6¹/₂ x 9¹/₂in (16.5 x 24cm) fabric for
  nightdress
Same size of fabric for day dress
Broderie anglaise eyelet edging
Four small buttons
Narrow blue ribbon
Ric-rac braid
Embroidery threads
Jersey fabric for hair
Polyester toy filling

Preparation
1 Trace the pattern on folded tracing paper, joining the pieces where indicated. Open the pattern and retrace to obtain the complete outline for each doll. Note that the pattern for the girl doll has a skirt outline while the boy doll pattern has a straight line on the body edge. Put in all marks, words and letters. Cut out the pattern.

MAKING THE DOLLS
Boy doll
2 Cut the pink fabric for the head in half.

3 **Sleepy-head side:** With right sides together, join the long edge of one strip of head fabric to pyjama fabric. Press seam towards darker toned fabric. Pin the pattern on the right side of the joined fabric with dotted lines A-B on the seam. Cut out ³/₈in (9mm) from the pattern for the seam allowance.

4 **Wide-awake side:** Join other strip of head fabric to shirt fabric in the same way. Join the trousers fabric to the shirt fabric, adjusting the seam allowance on the shirt strip. Pin the pattern to the joined strips with dotted lines A-B and C-D on seams. Cut out adding ³/₈in (9mm) seam allowance all round.

5 With right sides facing place front and back together. Leaving small gap in seam to turn, stitch all round. Snip into curves, turn to right side. Stuff evenly, close the opening.

Girl doll
6 Cut the pink head fabric in half. Cut the legs fabric across the width, to give two strips 3 x 9¹/₂in (7.5 x 24cm).

7 **Sleepy-head side:** Join the head piece to the nightdress fabric, adjusting the seam allowance on nightdress strip as necessary so that the finished width will correspond to the pattern. Pin the pattern to the fabric and cut out as for the boy doll.

8 **Wide-awake side:** Join and cut out as for the sleepy-head side.

9 Join and finish the two sides as for the boy doll, placing pieces right sides together, then stitching and stuffing.

Adapting patterns

The trace-off doll pattern can also be used to make a simple two piece clutch toy. These are ideal for small children and take very little time to make. Trace the shape on folded greaseproof paper and cut out. Open the pattern and pin to doubled printed cotton fabric. Cut out 1/4in (6mm) from the pattern edges. Cut 4 fabric circles for ears using a large coin for a template, again cutting 1/4in (6mm) from the edges. Stitch the ears together in twos, right sides facing, leaving about 1/2in (12mm) open. Turn right side out and stuff lightly. Pin the ears to the head on the right side of one body piece. Baste and then place the other body piece on top, right sides facing. Stitch all round, leaving a gap between the legs. Turn right side out, stuff the toy, close the gap. Embroider two round eyes and a smiling mouth in stem stitch.

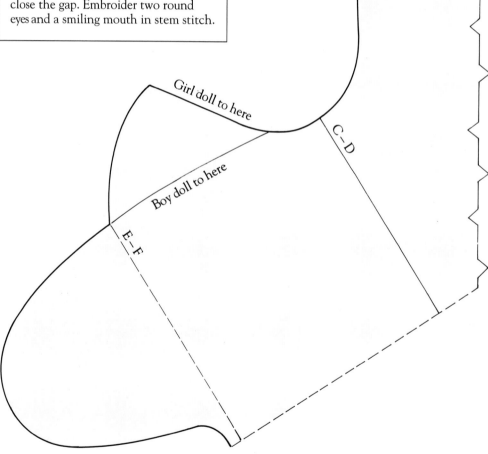

Girl doll to here

Boy doll to here

C–D

E–F

**Trace-off pattern for the Two-faced dolls.
Join pieces where indicated with arrows**

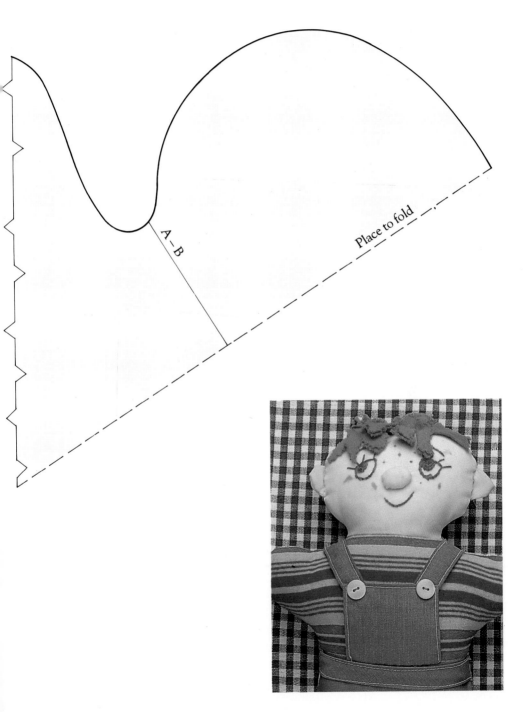

A – B

Place to fold

10 Faces: For a snub nose cut an oval of fabric 1 x 1¹/₂in (2.5 x 3.5cm), gather round the outside and draw up a little. Insert stuffing and stitch the nose to the head. Make an ear from two pieces of pink fabric each 1 x 1¹/₂in (2.5 x 3.5cm). With right sides facing cut them in a scallop shape, join with a ¹/₄in (6mm)seam, turn to right side. Make two the same. Sew to the side of the head tucking in raw straight edges as you sew. Embroider the boy's features in blue stem and straight stitches (see picture). Embroider the girl's features in pink thread. Freckles are indicated with dots of brown felt-tipped pen.

11 Hair: Cut strips of jersey fabric with pinking shears. For the boy doll, cut strips in 4in (10cm) pieces, tie a knot in the middle, sew the knot to the head. For the girl doll, gather the strips down the middle, pull up and sew to the head. Sew a ribbon bow in the girl doll's hair.

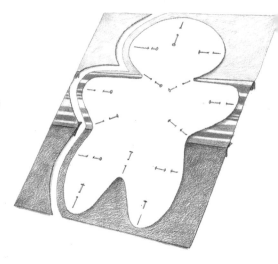

Wide-awake boy doll: pin the paper pattern to the joined fabric strips

Finishing

12 Sew ric-rac braid around the hem of the girl doll's day dress. Decorate with embroidery stitches (see picture). Sew on buttons as shown.

13 On the sleepy-head side, sew broderie anglaise eyelet edging around the nightdress neck and thread 9mm (³/₈in) blue ribbon through. Sew on buttons.

Cut ¹/₂in (12mm)-wide jersey strips into 4in (10cm) pieces and tie in a knot. Sew knots to the boy doll's head

14 On the boy doll's wide-awake side, cut a 1in (2.5cm) strip for a waistband, turn a hem to the wrong side all round and stitch across the waist. Cut a 2in (5cm) square of the same fabric, turn and press the edges, stitch and then sew above the waistband for a bib front. Cut fabric strips for the shoulder straps, turn and press the edges, top stitch and sew behind the bib to the shoulders. Sew on buttons.

15 Cut a 6 x 1in (15 x 2.5cm) strip of the pyjama fabric, press a narrow hem to the wrong side all round, top stitch and sew to the front of the sleepy-head side. Sew on three buttons.

If you would prefer to make a doll without having another face on the reverse, simply make up the front, then the back as instructed, but omit any buttons etc that indicate it is the alternative front view. Instead of embroidering the alternative face work the doll's hair all over the back head.

Frog prince

This clever upside-down doll is inspired by a popular fairy story in which a prince was turned into a frog by a wicked wizard, and was then transformed into a prince again by the kiss of a beautiful princess.

Materials

Soft drink can approximately 6in (15cm) long and 2³/4in (7cm) in diameter
9 x 6in (23 x 15cm) piece of lining fabric
10 x 6in (25 x 15cm) piece of flesh coloured felt
9in (23cm) square of emerald felt
9in (23cm) square of light green felt
20 x 10in (50 x 25cm) piece of green cotton fabric
36 x 12in (90 x 30cm) piece of fabric for prince's garment
20 x 16in (51 x 40cm) of blue fabric (pond)
1yd (90cm) white ric-rac braid
1yd (90cm) green ric-rac braid
Scraps of red, dark pink, yellow and white felt
Polyester toy filling
Yellow knitting wool for hair
Silver paper, small piece of stiff card, gold paper
Large sequin
Scrap of broderie anglaise
Embroidery threads
Four small dress weights (or coins)

Preparation

1 Trace the patterns, joining pieces where indicated. Put in all marks, words and letters. Cut out the pattern pieces.

2 Wrap the lining fabric widthways round the can overlapping the edges and glue in place.

3 Cut a piece of flesh-coloured felt 6 x 8³/4in (15 x 22cm) and a piece of light green felt the same size. Place the shorter edges of each piece together and oversew. Place the covered can lengthways on the felt, overlap the long edges and sew in place. The seam is the centre back.

4 Stuff the projecting felt at each end firmly to make the heads. Run a gathering thread round each end and draw up. Run another gathering thread just above the can rim at both ends and draw up a little for the necks.

5 Cut the front and back bodies and two upper arms from emerald felt. Cut two underarms from light green felt. Cut one front head from light green felt to dotted line on the pattern. Cut one mouth from red felt. For eyes cut two red and two yellow felt ovals each ³/4in x ¹/2in (18 x 12mm) and two slightly larger ovals in white felt. Cut two lily pads from green cotton and five water lilies from white felt. Cut two fronts and two backs of the skirt shape from blue cotton for the lily pond (and the prince's skirt).

MAKING THE DOLL
Frog

6 **Eyes:** Sew the white felt ovals to the front frog's head (see picture) then sew yellow and red ovals on top (see the picture), with two or three yellow stitches in the centres of the red ovals.

7 **Head:** Stitch the darts on the back body. With right sides facing, sew the front head to the back body round the sides. Turn to the right side and place the joined pieces on the light green felt end of the covered can. Insert a little stuffing under the domed parts of the head, then oversew the sides of the back in place, from the corners of the mouth downwards.

Patterns for the Frog Prince body, head,
mouth and arm. Join pieces where indicated.

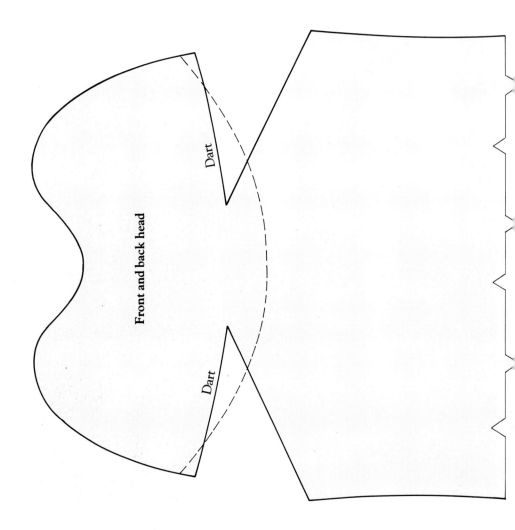

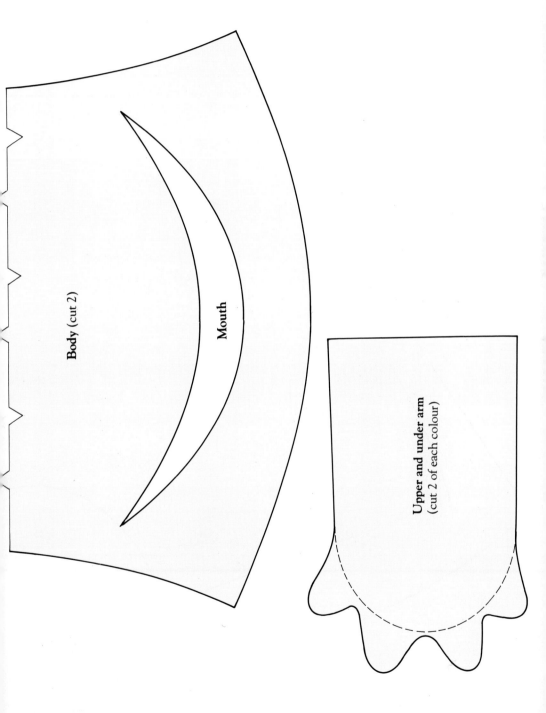

Body (cut 2)

Mouth

Upper and under arm
(cut 2 of each colour)

Trace-off patterns for the skirt and lily
pond, the lily pad, the Prince's sword and
the water lilies.

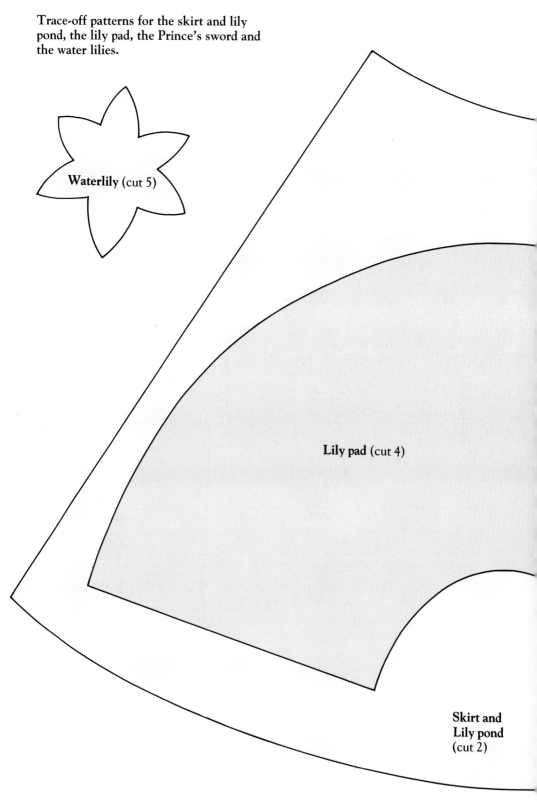

Waterlily (cut 5)

Lily pad (cut 4)

**Skirt and
Lily pond
(cut 2)**

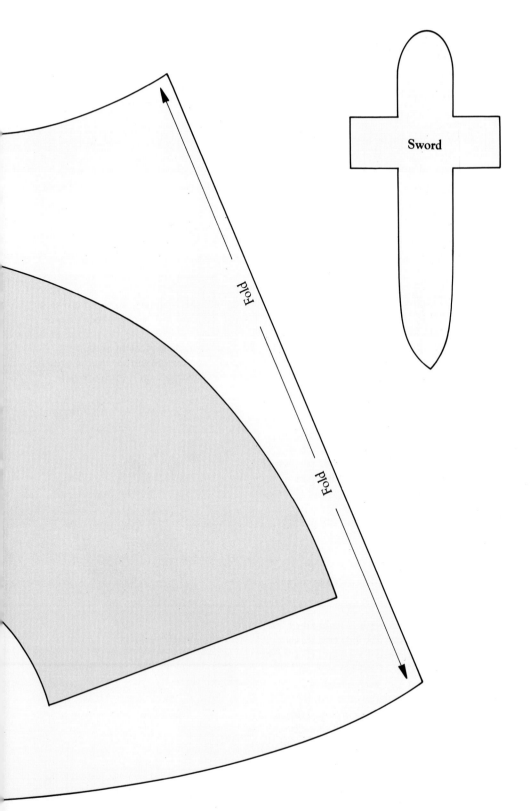

Fold

Fold

Sword

8 Oversew the upper edge of the mouth to the lower curve of the front head, then sew the lower edge of the mouth in place. Make a small crown from gold paper and stitch to the frog's head between the eyes.

9 **Lily pond skirt:** Join one front and one back of blue cotton skirt and stitch lengths of white ric-rac here and there for ripples. Hand sew green ric-rac braid round the outer edge.

10 Match the waist edges, oversew together and run a gathering thread next to the oversewing. Slip over the doll, draw up the thread and sew the waist to the seam of the bodices.

11 **Arms:** Place upper and under arms together in pairs, with straight upper edges even, and machine-stitch (or backstitch) together $1/8$in (3mm) from the edge leaving the straight edge open. Insert a weight in each, stuff lightly. Oversew raw edges together, oversew to bodice, level with neck gathering.

12 **Lily pad:** Join pieces for the lily pad as for the skirt, slip on the frog and catch in place just above the lily pond skirt. Stitch a green ric-rac belt just above the lily pad. Trace a pattern from the trace-off lily shape and cut four lilies from white felt. Catch the lilies to the skirt and lily pad, with a few orange stitches in the centre.

Prince

13 Cut and complete the prince's bodice as for the frog.

14 **Legs:** Cut two trouser legs from fabric each 6 x $3^{1}/4$in (15 x 8cm). Cut two shoes from dark pink felt, each 4 x $1^{1}/4$in (10 x 3cm). Place the edges of the trousers and shoes together and join with a narrow seam. Fold right sides facing and stitch round the shoe, curving the corners. Turn right side out, stuff the lower half of each leg only. Cut small scallop-shaped pieces of flesh-coloured felt and sew to the fronts of both shoes. Sew the tops of the legs to the front of the prince's waist.

15 **Jacket skirt:** Complete and attach as for the lily pad (see steps 9 and 10 for the frog).

16 **Arms:** Make and attach arms as for the frog.

17 Trace the pattern for the sword on stiff card and glue silver paper to both sides of the blade. Cover the hilt with coloured paper or ribbon. Sew to the prince's right hand.

18 **Features:** Cut two $1/2$in (12mm) circles of blue felt for the eyes and sew to the face, halfway down the head. Embroider the nose in straight stitches and the mouth in stem stitch. Make the prince's hair from knitting wool. Make a gold paper crown as for the frog and sew to the prince's head.

19 Gather a small piece of broderie anglaise for a cravat and sew to the prince's front. Sew a large sequin in the middle.

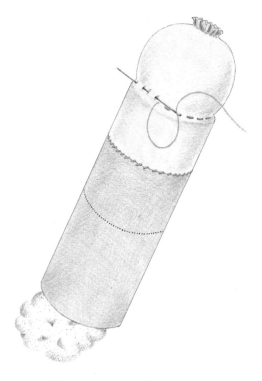

To make the heads, gather the projecting felt at the ends, stuff, then gather up the neck

Ballerina

The easy method of making this doll can be adapted to dolls of any size. The basic body is constructed of fabric-covered foam. With the addition of a wand, the ballerina becomes a fairy doll.

Materials

45 x 20in (115 x 50cm) piece of flesh-coloured fabric
31 x 20in (80 x 50cm) piece of 1/4in (6mm)-thick flame-retardant poly-foam
31in (80cm) of 4in (10cm)-wide lace
15in (40cm) of 11/4in (3cm)-wide lace
Scraps of satin fabric
8in (20cm) of 1/4in (6mm)-diameter dowel
51/2in (14cm) of 1/8 (3mm)-diameter dowel
1 large sequin, several tiny sequins
1yd (90cm) of narrow satin ribbon
4in (10cm) of glitter trim
Rayon thread (for hair)
Sewing cotton, pink embroidery thread
Scraps of white and blue felt

Note: Cut fabric for the body on the cross throughout.

Preparation

1 Body: The left arm and the left leg, and the right arm and the right leg are each made in one piece from a covered roll of foam.

2 Cut two pieces of foam each 19 x 9in (48 x 23cm) and two pieces of fabric each 20 x 12in (50 x 30cm). Fold the foam in half lengthways and roll up, not too firmly. Pin the long edge in place and then over-sew using large stitches to hold it in place.

3 For one leg and arm press 1/4in (6mm) to wrong side along one long edge of a fabric piece. Place it on a flat surface and roll it round a foam tube so that the folded edge of the fabric neatly overlaps the raw edge, and 12mm (1/2in) of fabric projects at either end. Hem the folded edge. Turn in the raw edges of fabric at the ends, gather

and draw up. Make the other leg and arm in the same way.

4 Head: Cut a piece of foam 19 x 12in (48 x 30cm) and a piece of fabric 101/2 x 5in (27 x 13cm). Fold the foam evenly into three lengthways. Roll up firmly widthways, pin and baste the edge as for the legs and arms. The roll should have a circumference of about 10in (25cm).

5 Insert the dowel into the centre of the roll so that 43/4in (12cm) projects below it.

6 Cover the head with fabric as before. With doubled thread gather round the raw edges, draw up tightly at the top of head and draw up more loosely at the neck end. Try to draw up the gathers so that the area of the face is smooth.

MAKING THE DOLL

7 Fold each leg and arm tube so that the fold is one third from the end. These are the shoulders. Catch the folds in place with doubled thread. Place the projecting dowel between the two body pieces and sew the tubes together, taking stitches from side to side to enclose the dowel.

8 Catch the base of the head to the shoulders. Run a gathering thread around each arm 11/4in (3cm) from the end and draw up, for wrists. Take a stitch along the upper edge of the hands to represent division of thumbs.

9 For the body cover cut a piece of pink fabric 61/2 x 51/2in (17 x 14cm). Cut slits for armholes. Press a 1/4in (6mm) hem to the wrong side on one short edge. With

right sides facing fold the fabric so that the short edges overlap. Join the shoulder seams, taking 1/8in (3mm) seam allowance and making each shoulder seam 3/8in (9mm) long. Turn to right side. Slip on to the doll over the arms, overlap the edges down the centre back and hem down the folded edge. With a needle point push the raw edges of the armholes to the inside and catch down.

10 Catch the body cover together between the doll's legs. Backstitch across the legs on a level with the base of the dowel, to enable the doll to sit down.

Hair and face

11 Wind yarn round a piece of card 9in (23cm) wide and cut from the card. Sandwich the strands between 2 layers of tissue and machine-stitch along the centre. Sew the hair all round the face. Tie into a pony tail. For the eyes, cut two circles of blue felt and two circles of white felt each 1/2in (12mm) diameter. Sew a blue felt circle overlapping a white circle. Work two or three tiny white stitches in the centre of each for highlight, sew to face. Add blue straight stitches for eyelashes.

12 Work a small fly stitch in pink thread for the mouth. Fold a piece of tissue to a point, brush lightly in lipstick and dot the cheeks. Smudge the dots into each other.

Doll's clothes

Unless otherwise stated, cut all fabric on the straight grain of fabric.

13 Make the bodice as for the body cover. For sleeves, cut the narrower lace in half, join the short edges and gather along the straight edges. Slip over the arms and catch to the bodice. Catch the inner arms to the sides of the bodice in the desired attitude.

14 Cut the satin underskirt 31 x 4in (80 x 10cm). Join the short edges and turn a narrow hem along one long edge. Gather the remaining edge, slip on to the doll and catch to the base of the bodice. Complete the lace overskirt in the same way and attach. Glue sequins to the lace skirt.

15 For shoes, cut two pieces of satin on the cross 2in (5cm) square. Press 1/4in (6mm) to the wrong side on one edge of each. With right sides together fold the fabric in two. Taking a 1/8in (3mm) seam, join the edges starting at A and continue from B to C (see diagram). Gather B-C. Turn to right side. Slip the shoes on the feet so that opening is at front With a needle point, push the raw edges to the inside, catch the shoes to the feet. Tie narrow ribbon next to upper edge of shoe and finish with a bow at centre front.

16 To complete the doll, tie a sash of narrow ribbon round the lower edge of the bodice and catch a piece of glittering trim round the neck of the bodice. For a fairy doll, make a wand by winding ribbon round a 6in (15cm) piece of thin stick and glue the ends to secure. Glue a large sequin to one end.

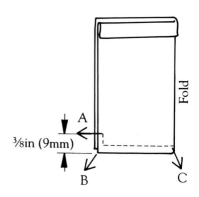

Diagram for cutting the shoes fabric

Push raw edges to the inside and catch to the foot with tiny stitches

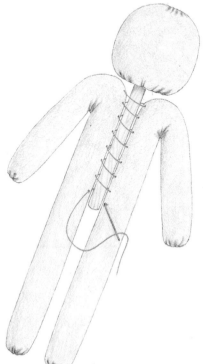

Work stitches from side to side of the body pieces to hold the dowel securely

If flesh-coloured fabric for doll's bodies is not easily available, pure cotton white jersey or woven fabric can be dyed with a cold-water dye. Cold tea will also tint fabric to a suitable colour. Make the tea very strong. Dampen the fabric and wring out to remove excess water. Steep in the tea and move the fabric around occasionally to get an even absorption. Lift the fabric out, wring, dry and press.

Sweet Sue

This is a traditional rag doll, very simply made and with a complete wardrobe of clothes, including a party dress and two pairs of shoes. It stands about 21in (53cm) high.

Materials for doll
45 x 8in (120 x 20cm) of flesh-coloured cotton
1lb (500g) of polyester toy filling
2oz (50g) of DK knitting wool
Scraps of blue and pink felt
Embroidery threads
Small piece of stiff card

Materials for clothes
20 x 9in (51 x 23cm) dress fabric
18in (45cm) of 3in (7.5cm)-wide broderie anglaise
13in (33cm) of 2in (5cm)-wide broderie anglaise
6in (15cm) square of felt
24in (60cm) narrow ribbon
2 beads or buttons (for shoes)
Embroidered motif (for hair)
10in (25cm) of narrow elastic

Preparation
1 Trace the body patterns (pages 34-35). Cut out the pieces and pin to fabric. All pieces are cut out with 3/8in (9mm) added for seam allowance. Cut four bodies, and two legs. Position the pieces for the head and the head gusset on the bias of the fabric and cut two side heads and one head gusset. Mark the front head on each piece and the middle of the head gusset. Mark the stitching lines for the arms on the body pieces.

Making the doll
2 **Body:** Join two body pieces along the centre front seam, right sides facing. Press the seam open. Still with right sides facing, stitch all round the body, leaving the neck edge open. Snip into curves almost up to the stitching line. Turn right side out.

3 **Head:** Join the side heads to the head gusset, matching fronts. Turn right side out. Turn in the seam allowance on the neck edge and baste in place.

4 **Legs:** Join the side seams and fold so that the seam is at centre back. Mark the fabric with curved lines. Stitch round, taking 3/8in (9mm) seams, snip into curves. Turn to right side.

5 **Body stuffing:** Stuff the arms firmly and smoothly. When stuffing the hands, insert only a very little stuffing at a time and press it into place with a knitting needle or tweezers. Stuff a little less firmly when you are near the stitching line for the arm joints. Sew or machine stitch along the lines (see pattern). Continue to stuff body.

6 **Head stuffing:** Stuff firmly and smoothly. Turn in the seam allowance at the neck and baste.

7 **Legs stuffing:** Stuff firmly, but insert a little less stuffing at the top of the legs. Turn in the seam allowance at the top of the legs then oversew.

8 Oversew the legs to the body, matching the centre seams on the body to the inner join of the legs. Pin the head to the body, matching centres then oversew in place inserting any extra stuffing at neck as you sew.

9 **Hair:** For the short curls, cut a piece of stiff card 6 x 2in (15 x 5cm). Cut out the centre so that the remainder of the card is 1/4in (6mm) wide. Wind wool round the card and machine-stitch down the centre. Slide the wool from the card. Make several lengths and sew to the head, starting at the crown of the head and working round in a

spiral. Bring the curls over the front of the head. Sew the decorative embroidery motif to one side of the head.

10 Face: Cut two blue felt circles for eyes and two pink circles for cheeks, each 1/2in (12mm) diameter. Oversew to the head placing the eyes about 1 1/4in (3cm) up from the neck seam and 3/8in (9mm) apart. Position the cheeks to one side of the eyes and sew in place. Embroider the mouth in stem stitch using 3 strands of thread together, working on level with the cheeks. Embroider eyelashes with 2 strands of thread and take two or three tiny stitches in white in the centre of each eye for highlights.

11 Sew a flower-shaped lace motif to the doll's middle (see picture).

Making the clothes
12 Panties: Join the short ends of the narrower broderie anglaise. Turn and stitch a narrow hem along one straight long edge to make a casing, leaving a small gap. Run elastic through. Close the gap in the seam. Catch the scalloped edges together in the centre for the division of the legs. For the petticoat, join the wider piece of broderie anglaise, as you did for the panties. Make a casing on one long edge, run a ribbon or tape through and draw up.

13 Dress: Cut two pieces of dress fabric, one 20 x 6in (51 x 15cm) and the other 20 x 2 1/2in (51 x 6cm). Oversew one long edge on each. To find the position for the armholes fold the larger piece of fabric so that the raw edges are touching, press along the folded edges, then place pins 1 3/8in (3.5cm) in from the folds on both neatened edges.

14 With right sides facing join pieces with 1/4in (6mm) seam, leaving spaces between pins for armholes. Press the seam open. Turn in a narrow hem along the short edges and along the remaining long edges so that the upper fabric is 1 1/2in (4cm) wide and lower is 4 1/4in (11cm) wide. For the frill, cut a piece of fabric 32 x 2 1/2in (80 x 6cm), and neaten the long edges. Gather

Stitch the side seam, so that it lies centre back of the leg. Stitch the foot in a curve, clip into the seam allowance. The sock and shoe are made in the same way

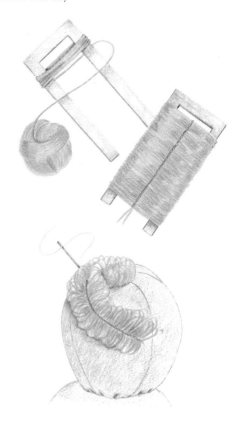

Cut the centre from a card strip, wind wool round and machine-stitch across the middle. Slip wool from card for the doll's short curls

Sweet Sue's underwear is simply made and she has a
discreet flower motif sewn to her middle

along the centre and draw up the frill to fit the dress. Sew in place over the hem on the right side. Run ribbon through the neck hem, then sew a ribbon bow to the centre front.

15 Socks and shoes: Cut 2 pieces of jersey fabric for each sock, $4^3/4$ x $2^1/4$in (12 x 6cm). Join as for the lower ends of the legs. Turn a narrow hem at the top of each sock. For shoes, cut 2 felt strips each $5^1/4$ x $1^1/2$in (13 x 4cm). Join as for the socks. Cut a D-shaped portion from the front of each shoe. Slip on the socks, then the shoes. Stitch a button or bead to the shoe front for decoration.

16 A complete wardrobe of dresses in different colours and fabrics can be made

from the dress instructions. A broderie anglaise nightdress, made in the same way, also makes a pretty addition to the rag doll's wardrobe.

17 For a negligeé, choose a thin fabric, make up the dress pattern and slip onto the doll back to front, over the nightdress. Finish the neckline with a large, satin bow.

If you prefer, embroider the doll's hair using chunky knitting wool. Start with a knot, and take a stitch. Without pulling the wool right through, take a back stitch, leaving a loop. Make loops all over the head.

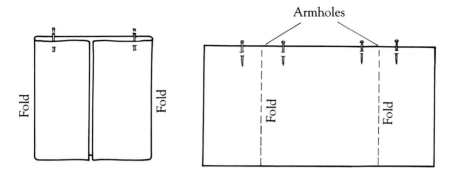

Above: diagrams for the basic doll's dress. The party dress is made in the same way as the day dress, with the addition of pretty trimmings

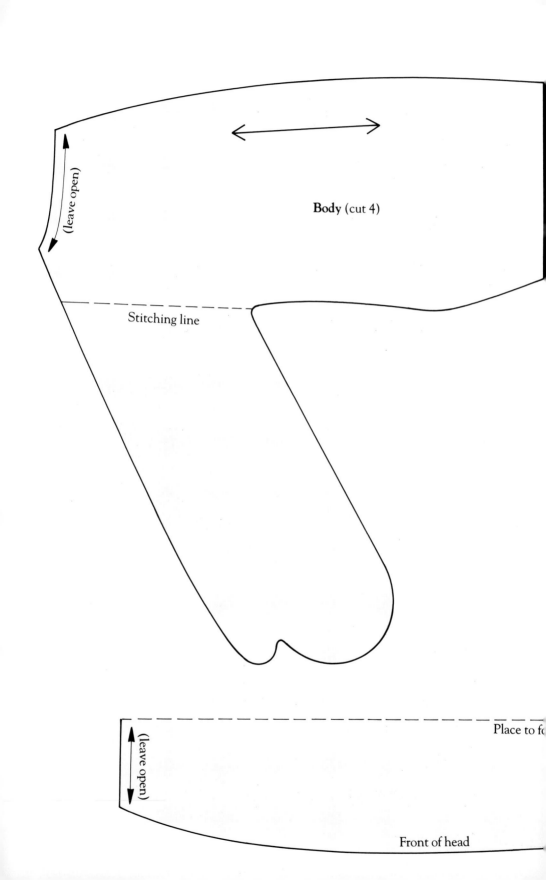

Body (cut 4)

(leave open)

Stitching line

Place to fo

(leave open)

Front of head

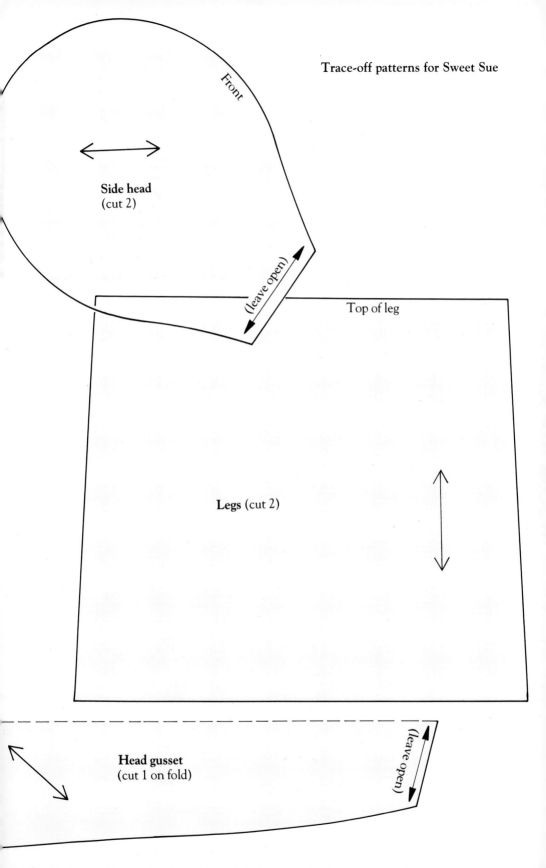

Trace-off patterns for Sweet Sue

Front

Side head
(cut 2)

(leave open)

Top of leg

Legs (cut 2)

Head gusset
(cut 1 on fold)

(leave open)

Sock gnome

Here's an idea for a doll which is quick and easy to make from scrap materials. The idea can be adapted for any rag doll.

Materials

Pair of short ankle socks (or one knee sock)
An old T-shirt (or lightweight jersey fabric)
Medium-sized round bead
Two ³/₈in (9mm)- diameter black buttons
2 coloured buttons of any size
Red stranded embroidery thread
Polyester toy filling
Small amount of knitting wool

Preparation

1 If you are using ankle socks cut off one of the feet for the body. For the legs and arms, trim off the sock leg above the heel and divide it lengthways in two, then cut the leg of the other sock in the same way. If you are using a knee sock cut off the foot, then divide the leg equally into four. Retain a heel for a beard whichever length of sock you are using.

Making the doll

2 Stuff the sock foot for the body and temporarily pin the open end together.

3 For the nose, cover the bead with a circle of sock fabric. Slide it under the body fabric until it is about 2in (5cm) below the end of the sock toe and positioned in the centre. Work stem stitch with red embroidery thread round the bead to emphasize it, stitching through the covering fabric as you work. Remove the pins from the stuffed sock foot and oversew the open end to close.

4 Insert a little stuffing into the heel piece which was put aside for the beard and oversew the raw edges together, then stitch the beard in a curve below the nose. Embroider a smiling mouth in red stem stitch above the beard. Sew the buttons for eyes either side of the nose.

Cut the foot from a knee sock, keep the heel for the beard, divide the leg into 4 pieces

5 For the hair, cut a strip of white jersey 1¼in (3cm) wide. With right sides facing, fold in half along the length and join the long edges taking a ¼in (6mm) seam. Turn to the right side. Sew in loops round the head just above the level of the eyes .

6 Arms and legs: With right sides facing, join the long edges of each arm and leg piece. Turn to the right side and re-fold so that the seam lies down the centre Seam across one short end on each piece. Stuff two tubes for the legs until they are about 1¼in (3cm) shorter than the length of the body. Gather across just above the stuffing, then draw up the threads and secure.

7 Trim the excess fabric to ½in (12mm) above the gathering. Turn over the edges and oversew. Oversew the legs to the lower edge of the body so that they swing when the doll is held in the hand.

8 Stuff the arms until they are about three-quarters of the length of the legs, then finish as for the legs. Sew them to the sides of the body about half way down its length.

Clothes
9 Use a T-shirt sleeve for the cap, or make a tube from a piece of jersey fabric 7 x 5in (17.5 x 12.5cm). Gather the top and add a wool tassel. Stitch to the head just above the hair.

10 For the trousers, cut two 6¼in (16cm) squares of jersey. For leg seams fold each square in half with right sides facing and oversew the edges for 5in (12.5cm). Join the remainder of the corresponding edges together for centre front and back seams. Run a gathering thread round the waist, slip the trousers on the doll and draw up the thread to fit. Catch the waist to the doll's body and cut a waist band from fabric to match the cap. Turn in the raw edges and stitch over the top of the trousers. Stitch a button to the centre front of the waistband.

11 Make a paper pattern for the jacket by drawing a 7½in (19cm)- diameter circle with a hole 2¾in (7cm) diameter in the centre. Cut this in jersey fabric and slit across the width for the front opening. Oversew the edges to neaten. Place on the doll just over the top of the arms and turn back the edges of the front opening as necessary. Catch the jacket to the doll at centre front and round the neck. Catch the edges together underneath the arms to form sleeves.

12 Stitch a button to the neck opening of the jacket.

Sew the white jersey strips in loops round the head, just above the level of the eyes

---

Sock dolls
All kinds of dolls can be made with a pair of socks, using the toe for the head and the leg for the body. Legs and arms can be made from the second sock leg. Use a pale coloured, plain sock for the head, then a striped or spotted sock for the body, arms and legs. Sock dolls, if stuffed with washable polyester wadding, are ideal playthings for young children. They can be made to any size and quite big dolls can be made with a pair of wool tights or stockings. Always wash socks, stockings and tights carefully and never use any for doll making that are not colourfast.

Happy clown

This is a quick version of a doll made from patchwork Suffolk puffs.
The limbs are strung on elastic and the basis of the
body is a wooden spoon.

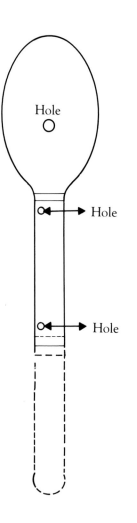

Hole

O

Hole

Hole

Materials

Size: 15in (38cm) high
Large wooden spoon
26 x 8in (66 x 20cm) of orange fabric
18½ x 8½in (47 x 22cm) blue fabric
20 x 8in (51 x 20cm) flowered fabric
Small piece of yellow jersey
Scraps of black, red and white felt
Small piece of medium thick card
Orange wool (for hair)
Five black wooden beads or small buttons
1 large red bead
Black and white stranded embroidery
    threads
Polyester toy filling
26in (66cm) narrow, flat elastic

Preparation

1 Saw off the handle of the wooden spoon
4½in (11.5cm) below the bowl. Drill two
holes approx ⅛in (3mm) in diameter
through from side to side, one just below
the bowl and the other ½in (12mm) above
the end. Drill another hole half way down
the bowl of the spoon (to attach the bead
for the nose later).

Saw off the spoon handle and drill holes for the arms,
nose bead and for the legs

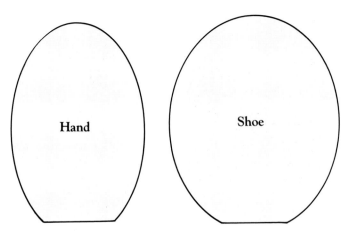

Hand

Shoe

2 To make a pattern for the head covering lay the bowl of the spoon on paper and draw round the bowl and handle up to the first hole. Cut out the pattern. Fold the yellow jersey doubled and pin the pattern to it so that the jersey stretch runs from side to side. Cut out with $^3/8$in (9mm) seam allowance all round.

Making the doll
3 Stitch round the curved edges of the head, turn to the right side and slip over the spoon. Slide stuffing between the jersey and the concave bowl of the spoon to shape the back of the head. Wind thread round the jersey to fasten it to the spoon, just above the upper drilled hole.

4 Arms: Cut the elastic into two equal lengths and thread one piece through the upper hole.

5 For the upper arms, cut two pieces of orange fabric each 7 x 5in (18 x 12.5cm). Neaten the long edges. With right sides facing, join the short ends taking $^1/4$in (6mm) seams. Turn to the right side. Run a gathering thread round one end of each tube. Slip the gathered ends over the elastic on either side of the handle, draw up the thread as tightly as possible and secure.

6 Stuff the upper arms lightly round the elastic, then run gathering threads round the remaining ends and draw up so that the elastic is left protruding.

7 For the arm ruffs, cut two pieces of blue fabric each 8$^1/2$ x 3in (21 x 7.5cm). Join each into 3in (7.5cm) tubes and gather as for the upper arms then slip over the protruding ends of elastic and stuff as before.

8 Finish the lower ends of each tube in the same way, first pinning the ends of elastic to the outside of the fabric so that they do not disappear into the stuffing.

9 Trace the pattern for the hands on to card and cut them out, then make a

Suffolk Puff toys
Suffolk puffs can be used to make amusing dolls of all kinds. Make a soft head and from this stitch on a doubled length of elastic, the loop at the bottom. Thread Suffolk puffs on the doubled elastic for the body. Thread elastic through the loop and thread more puffs for the legs. Finish the ends with feet made of felt and card. Knot the elastic between the puffs, about where 'shoulders' would be, thread on more puffs for the arms. Finish at the ends with felt hands. Embroider the doll's face. Toys made from puffs are very flexible and make very good puppets. Attach strings to the hands and feet and knot the strings of the left hand and foot to the ends of a stick and right hand and foot strings to another stick.

Thread elastic through the upper hole for the arms. Slip the orange fabric tubes on to the elastic, gather to secure and stuff

41

covering for each from jersey as for the head and slip over the card shapes. Insert a little stuffing to pad out the hands. Push the end of the elastic inside one hand and trim the jersey level with the top of the card hands then oversew the edges to close, catching the elastic firmly in place. Adjust the length of the elastic if necessary so that the various parts of each arm fit snugly together, and fasten the remaining hand in place.

10 Legs: Thread the remaining elastic through the lower hole in the spoon handle.

11 Cut the upper legs and the leg ruffs to the same measurements as for the arms, using blue fabric for the upper legs and flowered fabric for the ruffs. The legs are made in the same way as the arms.

12 Trace the patterns for the feet and cut out twice in card and four times in black felt. Oversew a pair of black felt pieces together, sandwiching cards in between for each foot. Leave the straight edges of each open. Stuff and insert elastic as before.

13 Body: Cut orange fabric 16 x 8in (41 x 20cm). With right sides facing join short ends, taking 1/4in (6mm) seam allowance. Turn to right side. Turn in 1/4in (6mm) at top and bottom edges and run a gathering thread round each.

14 Slip the body over the spoon handle from the legs upwards to just below the arm's elastic. Draw up the upper gathering thread to fit the spoon handle, secure the thread and catch to the surplus jersey just below the bowl of the spoon.

15 Partly draw up the lower gathering thread and stuff the body very lightly. Draw up the thread so that the gathers fit around two of your fingers placed in the middle of them. Secure the thread. The end of the body should be below the lower end of the spoon handle. Catch the gap between the gathers together.

16 Neck ruff: Cut and join sufficient bias-cut strips of flowered fabric to give a length 23 x 4in (58 x 10cm). With right sides facing, fold in half lengthways and seam close to the edge, turn to the right side and join the short ends. Gather along the folded edge, slip on to the doll and draw up to fit the neck and catch in place.

17 Features, hair and hat: Sew the red bead securely to the front of the face for a nose, stitching through the hole drilled in the spoon and through the stuffing at the back of the head.

18 Trace the features from the pattern. Cut the mouth from red felt, and eye and mouth backings from white felt. Cut the eyes from black felt. Oversew the mouth to its backing and embroider a line of black stem stitch in the centre as shown in the pattern. Oversew the eyes to their backings and embroider white straight lines down the centre for highlights. Oversew the assembled features to the front of the face and embroider a fine line of black stem stitch all round them. Stitch narrow strips of black felt for eyebrows to the top of the eyes as shown in the picture.

19 For the hair, wind orange wool about seventeen times round three fingers and fasten the loops together by stitching wool round them. Sew the assembled loops to the head, starting at either side of the face, about half way down and continuing round the back on the same level.

20 Make a hat by cutting blue fabric 7 x 2 1/4 (18 x 6cm). With right sides facing join the short ends. Run a gathering thread round one edge, pull up tightly and secure. Turn to right side. Turn in 1/4in (6mm) on the other edge and sew the hat to the top of the head. Catch one side of hat in folds (see picture).

Finishing
21 Make five Suffolk puffs to decorate the doll. Draw a circle 2 3/4in (7cm) diameter on paper and use this as a pattern to cut

circles of flowered fabric. Run a gathering thread round the outer edge of each and draw up as much as possible. Secure the thread. With the gathered edge uppermost, catch one to each shoe front, one to the top of the hat and two to the body front. Sew a black bead or button in the centre of each Suffolk puff.

Trace the features patterns (below), cut from felt and oversew the mouth to the mouth backing. Oversew the eyes to the eyes backing. Oversew the features to the clown's face. Work black stem stitch all round to highlight the eyes and mouth

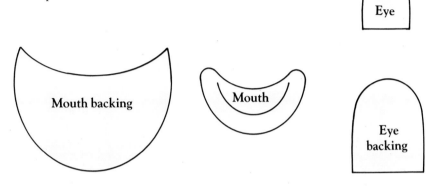

Eye

Mouth backing

Mouth

Eye backing

Cuddly rabbit

Here is a toy that will be a bedtime favourite. Make it from soft, fleecy fabric and stuff with a washable, polyester toy filling.

Materials
45 x 6in (112 x 15cm) of fluffy, washable fabric for head, ears and paws
7 x 6in (18 x 15cm) of pink fluffy fabric (for ear linings)
25 x 13in (64 x 33cm) of fluffy fabric for hood, sleeping bag and arms
Scraps of pink felt
Grey stranded embroidery thread
4 buttons
Polyester toy filling

Preparation
1 Trace the patterns for the lower front head, side head and ears. Cut out and use for patterns to cut fabric.

2 Allowing $1/4$in (6mm) seam allowance all round, cut two side heads, one lower head and two ears. Cut two paws pieces $51/2$ x $21/2$in (14 x 6cm) and a circle of fabric 4in (10cm)-diameter for the tail. Cut two pink ear linings.

3 For the sleeping bag, cut one front $101/4$ x 10in (26 x 25cm) and one back $101/4$ x $83/4$in (26 x 22cm), two arms each $51/2$ x 4in (14 x 10cm). Cut two strips for the sleeping bag hood, one $121/2$ x 3in (31 x 7.5cm), the other $121/2$ x $21/2$in (31 x 6cm).

Making the rabbit
4 **Head:** Pin and baste all seams before stitching. With right sides facing, stitch the darts on the side head pieces and then trim the seam back to $1/4$in (6mm). Stitch the lower head to the side heads, matching C-D. Join the side heads together round the remaining seam C-E. Turn to the right side. Stuff the head.

5 **Ears:** With right sides facing, join the outer ears to the linings. Turn right side out. Oversew the bottom, raw edges together. Fold the bottom edge, then stitch the ears to the head.

6 **Features:** Trace the nose shape and cut from pink felt. For the mouth, cut a pink felt strip $21/2$ x $1/4$in (60 x 6mm). Stitch the nose in place, centring it just below the place where the seams join and the curving upper edge.

7 Cut a $3/4$ x $1/4$in (18 x 6mm) strip of pink felt and stitch below the nose, then stitch the remainder of the strip in a curve. Embroider the closed eyelids in stem stitch (see picture).

8 **Arms:** With right sides facing, join a paw piece to each arm piece. Join the long edges of each assembled piece. Re-fold the tube so that the seam is in the centre, stitch rounded ends for the paws, then turn to the right side. Stuff lightly. Oversew the raw edges together.

9 **Sleeping bag:** Fold and pin a vertical pleat in the centre of the front bag piece, so that the front matches the back. Sew four buttons down the pleat. Pin the arms to the bag front, placing them $1/4$in (6mm) from the top edges.

10 With right sides facing, place the bag back on top. Stitch, enclosing the arms in the seam and leaving the upper edges open. Turn to the right side. Stuff lightly and run a gathering thread round the upper edge. Draw up to fit the neck and stitch in place.

11 **Hood:** With the right sides facing, baste the long edges of the hood pieces together. Fold 1in (2.5cm) on the narrower

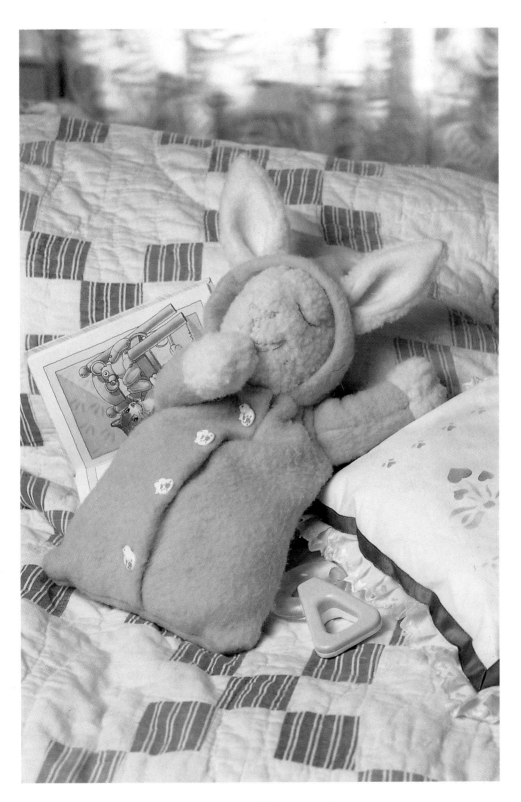

piece to the wrong side and catch in place. Fold the hood across the width, matching the short edges and join the centre back seam. Try the hood on the rabbit, marking the places where the ears will project through the front seam and stitch the remainder of the seam. Neaten the lower edge and run a gathering thread round. Draw up a little and catch in place to the neck.

Trace-off patterns for the Cuddly rabbit

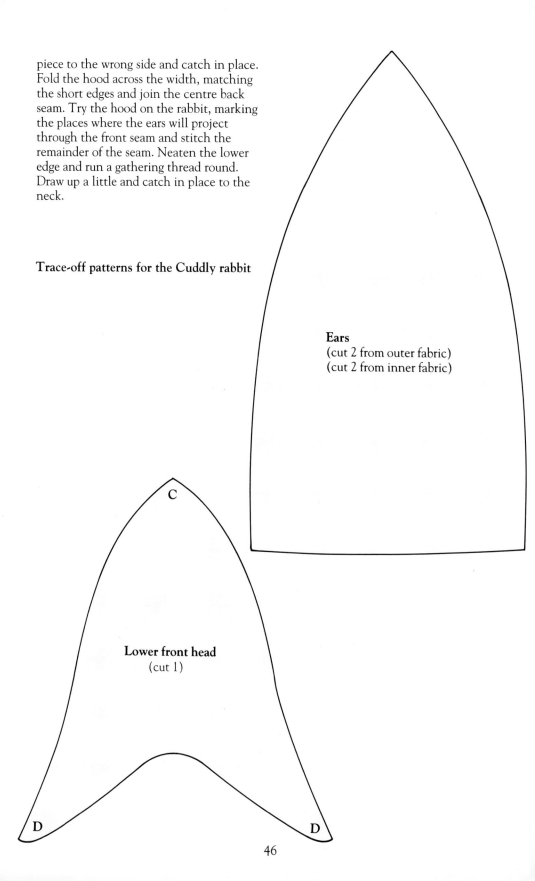

Ears
(cut 2 from outer fabric)
(cut 2 from inner fabric)

C

Lower front head
(cut 1)

D   D

Finishing

12 Curve the upper edges of the arms by running a gathering thread along them. Catch the tip of the right paw to the centre of the rabbit's mouth. Gather the outer edge of the tail. Draw up and insert stuffing, then sew to the centre of the back.

Nightie case
The cuddly rabbit can be adapted to make a small nightwear case. Cut the sleeping bag front into 2 pieces and turn a narrow hem on both cut edges. Insert an 8in (20cm) zip fastener, then finish the seam above and below the zipper. Continue as in stage 9, pinning the arms in place. Then continue with stage 10 but do not stuff the bag. If you prefer, you could work a button and loop fastening, or simply sew on a row of press fasteners and overlap the bag's front edges.

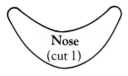

Nose
(cut 1)

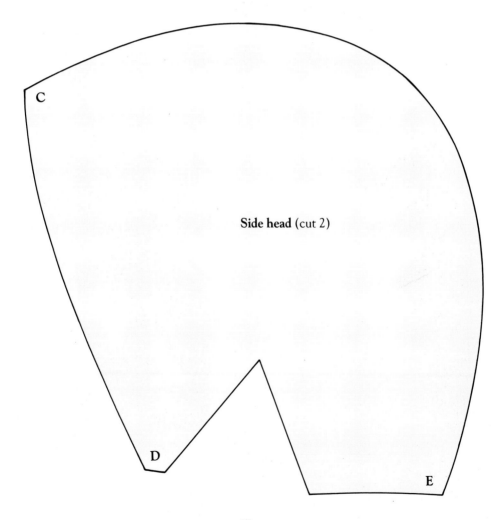

C

Side head (cut 2)

D

E

TWO

Useful Dolls

Message doll

Sew a label to the front of this floppy, cuddly doll and write a message on it such as 'Happy Birthday', 'Get Well Soon' or just 'I Love You'.

Materials
8 x 6½in (20 x 16.5cm) fabric for the doll's jersey
Two 6½in (16.5cm) squares fabric for trousers
15¾in (40cm) square of light- coloured scrap fabric
10¼in (26cm) square of flesh- coloured knitted fabric
Knitting wool for hair
Polyester toy filling
Scraps of blue and pink felt
Black, white and red embroidery threads
1 small bead
Strong sewing thread

Preparation
1 Place a large ball of stuffing in the centre of the light-coloured scrap fabric. When lightly compressed it should be the size of a large grapefruit. Gather up the fabric with the hand, further compressing the stuffing into a firm ball about 10in (25cm) in circumference. Wind thread round the gathered fabric to secure the ball. This makes the head.

2 To shape the head, wind strong thread first horizontally round the centre drawing in the sides of the ball, then vertically, flattening the top and sides. Sew the threads together where they cross. Pull down one horizontal thread to shape the back of the head. To position the nose, stitch the bead just below the horizontal thread at the centre front of the face.

3 Cut an 8in (20cm) circle of knitted fabric for the face. Run a gathering thread round the outside and put over the head. Pull up the gathering tightly towards the back of the head and secure the thread

Face and hair
4 Mark the position of the features, placing the eyes level with the horizontal line of thread. Cut two ³/₈in (9mm)- diameter circles of felt for the eyes and one for the mouth. Sew them in place. Work black straight stitches for the eyelashes and vertical straight stitches in black and white for the centres of the eyes. Work a fly stitch in red for the centre of the mouth. Lightly colour the cheeks with lipstick.

5 To make the hair, cut six 17¾in (45cm)-long strands of knitting yarn and tie them together with an overhand knot in the middle. Sew the knot to the front hairline. Repeat until the doll has a full head of hair working round the front and back of the head. Tie a length of knitting wool round to make a pony tail.

Clothes
6 **Sweater:** Fold the fabric in four and cut out a section under the arms . With ¼in (6mm) seams throughout, sew the underarms, then cut a slit at the centre top just big enough to pull through the excess fabric below the head. Stitch the sweater to the neck.

The method used for the Message doll's hair is very simple and effective and makes a pretty ponytail effect. To adapt the method for a boy doll, fold the yarn into a skein, then tie a knot in the middle. Sew the knots to the hair line and sew the loops to the crown of the head, so that the doll's head is completely covered.

7 Trousers: Fold the squares of trousers in half with right sides facing. Join centre back and front seams for 2in (5cm). Then stitch each inside leg seam. Neaten the waist and ankle seams. Gather the waist slightly and stitch the trousers to the sweater.

Hands and feet

8 Cut four 5in (12.5cm) circles of fabric. Run a gathering thread 1¼in (3cm) in from the edge of each circle, insert stuffing and draw up the thread, winding it round the excess fabric to form a wrist or ankle. Gather the wrists of the jumper round each hand and stitch into place. Add the feet to the trousers in the same way.

9 Write your message on a piece of white fabric and sew it to the front of the sweater.

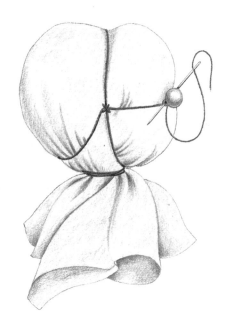

Position the nose by stitching a bead just below the horizontal thread at the centre front of the face

Sew blue felt eyes to the face and embroider lashes and pupils in straight stitches. Sew a pink felt mouth on and work a red fly stitch in the middle

Loving greetings
It's a good idea to make the message doll's greeting permanent, so that it can be kept for always. Choose your message with only 2 or 3 words. Write them on smooth fabric. Embroider the words in chain stitch. Using Bondaweb, mount the fabric on pelmet-weight Vilene (Pellon). Turn and glue the edges to the wrong side, then back the message with fabric or felt. Sew the rectangle to the doll's hands.

Tidy teddy

Teddy is quickly and simply made and is designed to hang from a door or a bed post. The back of the bear opens for storing nightclothes or small toys.

Materials

36 x 16in (91 x 40cm) piece of gingham
   fabric
12in (30cm) square of contrast cotton
36 x 16in (91 x 40cm) of thin, flame
   retardant foam sheeting
Scraps of white, blue and black felt
Black and white embroidery threads
2 buttons

Preparation

1 For the front body and lining pattern
draw the shape from the diagram, opposite
(bottom). For the front dungarees, redraw
the same pattern on another piece of
paper, fold the pattern in half vertically
and draw the upper edge of the dungarees
as shown in the second diagram (top
right). Cut out. For the pocket, draw a
rectangle 5 x 2³/₄in (13 x 7cm), fold in half
widthways and round off the lower edges

2 Draw a circle 7¹/₂in (19cm) diameter for
the head. Trace the patterns for ears and
paws. Cut out patterns.

3 Cut one front body and one lining,
adding ³/₈in (9mm) seam allowance all
round. Fold the body pattern in half
vertically and cut 2 pieces for the back
body,including the seam allowance but
adding 1¹/₄in (3cm) extra on the straight,
centre back edges.

4 Cut 2 front dungarees, 2 dungaree
pockets, 2 dungaree straps each 6¹/₄ x 2¹/₂
in (16 x 6cm), 2 heads, 4 ears and 8 paws.
From the foam cut 2 heads, 2 ears and 4
paws. Fold the front body pattern
horizontally 6³/₄in (17cm) above the
centre of the rounded lower edge and cut 1
foam piece to pad the lower body.

MAKING THE DOLL
Head

5 For the eyes, cut two white felt ovals
each 2 x 1¹/₂in (5 x 4cm) and sew to one
head piece (see picture). Cut two blue felt
eyes each 1³/₄in (4cm) diameter and two
black pupils ³/₈in (9mm) diameter and sew
to the white ovals with two or three white
stitches in the centre of the black felt.

Sew the dungaree straps in place, adding buttons for
decoration if liked

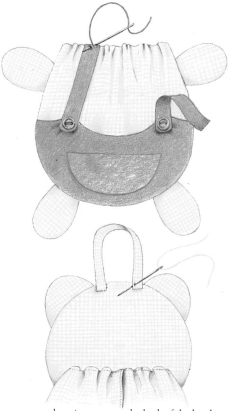

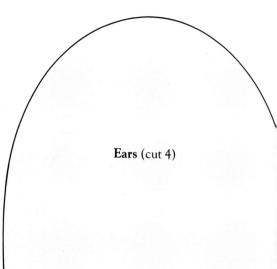

Sew a narrow hanging strap to the back of the head

Ears (cut 4)

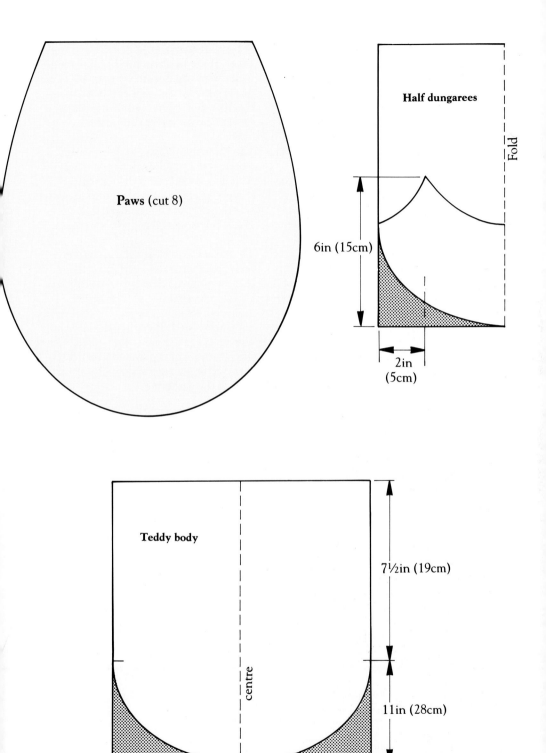

Paws (cut 8)

Half dungarees

Fold

6in (15cm)

2in
(5cm)

Teddy body

centre

7½in (19cm)

11in (28cm)

4¼in (11cm)

6 Cut a triangular black felt nose 1½ x 1in (4 x 2.5cm) and stitch between the eyes and slightly below them. Embroider the mouth in chain stitch.

7 With right sides facing, place two ears together and pin to a foam ear, matching the raw edges. Stitch all round the curved edges, leaving the straight edge open. Trim all seam allowances back to ¼in (6mm). Turn to right side. Make another ear in the same way.

8 With right sides facing, place the back and front head together and pin to two foam heads, matching the outer edges. Position the ears evenly on either side of head, mark places for the straight edges of the ears and remove them. Stitch all round the head, leaving the spaces for the ears unstitched and a gap for turning. Turn to the right side. Insert the ears, top stitch in place through all thicknesses. Close the remaining opening.

Body
9 Assemble the paws as for the ears.

10 Turn a narrow hem down the straight edges of two centre back pieces. Overlap the straight edges by ⅜in (9mm) and baste in place at top and bottom. Top stitch the overlap in place for 4⅜in (11cm) upwards from the rounded ends.

11 With right sides facing, place the front dungarees pieces together, stitch along the shaped upper edge, turn to right side and press. Assemble the pocket pieces in the same way, leaving a gap for turning. Turn to the right side and close the opening. Fold the pieces for the dungarees straps in half lengthways, stitch along the long edges taking a ¼in (6mm) seam. Turn to the right side and press with the seam in the centre. Turn in one short end. With contrasting thread top stitch along all joined edges on straps, dungarees front, and the straight edge of the pocket. Place the pocket in position on the dungarees front and top stitch the curved edge in place.

12 With right sides facing, place the dungarees on the front body, matching raw edges. Baste in place. Position the foam padding in place on the wrong side of the lining, then place front and back bodies together with right sides facing. Pin and baste them on top of the foam padding.

13 Arrange the paws so that they are evenly spaced and mark the positions. Stitch all round the body leaving the straight edges and the spaces for the paws unstitched. Turn to the right side, press. Insert the paws and top stitch in place.

14 Baste the raw, straight edges of the body together and neaten, then run a gathering thread through all thicknesses. Draw up to 4in (10cm). Place the dungarees straps to the shaped edge of the dungarees, stitch them in place, stitching buttons on at the same time if liked. Trim the raw edges of the straps to match the gathered upper edge and stitch to both ends of the gathering.

15 Place the teddy head overlapping the top of the body and sew the top of the body to the back of the head. To hang the toy make a narrow strap of gingham approx 8in (20cm) long and sew to the back of the head.

Working with fur fabrics
Fur fabrics are available in a wide variety of types, deep pile, shaggy, short pile etc. A lot of different colours and patterns are also available, from pastel shades, browns, beiges, to blacks and greys and some printed with designs to look like animal fur. It is inadvisable to buy fur fabric that is intended for clothing. Safety regulations concerning fabrics for children's toys should always be carefully observed, as some are highly flammable. Suitable fabrics usually have a safety label attached to the fabric bolt.

Doorstop Cat

Cat lovers will adore this handsome feline to prop open the door.
Or you might make two smaller ones and use them as book ends.

Materials
Container 6½in (16cm) tall and 3¾in
(9.5cm) diameter, with lid
22 x 11in (56 x 28cm) firm lining fabric
13 x 19in (33 x 48cm) of black knitted
jersey
11 x 9in (28 x 23cm) white jersey fabric
Scrap of orange felt for eyes
4in (10cm) square black felt
Stranded embroidery threads, black, white
and orange
Polyester toy filling
18in (45cm) fabric adhesive tape
Sand and pebbles (to weight the
container)
Thin string
Adhesive

Note: The original container used had
cardboard sides and a press-on polythene
lid. If you are unable to find one of the
suggested height you may be able to tape
two shorter containers together.

Preparation
1 Apply adhesive lightly to the bottom
half of the container sides. Cover the sides
of the container with polyester wadding, so
that the wadding is about 1in (2.5cm)
thick. Oversew the edges of the wadding
together.(The upper half of the wadding
should not be stuck to the container.)

2 Trace the patterns, joining pieces where
indicated with arrows. Put in all letters and
marks. Cut out.

3 Pin the lining pattern pieces to the
lining fabric and cut out adding a seam
allowance of ⅜in (9mm). With right sides
facing join the sides leaving the straight
edge open at the bottom and A-B at top.
Turn to the right side, press in a seam
allowance at the bottom.

4 Place the container so that the end with
the lid is at the bottom. Pull the lining
over the container so that the pressed-in
edge is level with the bottom of the
container.

5 Pin the lining to the wadding at the
front and back of the lower edge and stuff
the head firmly through the opening A-B.
Stuff the curved sides firmly. Close A-B.

6 Fold the black jersey fabric across the
width with right sides facing, and join the
long edges taking a ⅜in (9mm) seam. Fold
the tube flat so that the seam is at the
back. Stitch across one end ⅜in (9mm)
from the edge. Turn to the right side and
pull the fabric down over the container,
so that the seam is at the back.

7 Pull the cover well down and pin in
place at the lower edge of the cat, pushing
the pins through the lining and wadding.
The top corners will stick out to resemble
ears. Trim the lower edge of the fabric to
within 2in (5cm) of the bottom edge of the
container.

Contrast stripes
8 Trace the pattern for the white contrast
fabric (see pages 60-61, pattern for white
front). Put in the letters and marks. Cut out.

9 Pin the pattern to the white jersey and
cut out. Transfer the markings. Attach to
the cat body with a few pins at the front.
To shape the front, thread a strong needle
with button thread. Knot the end. Starting
from the inside of the container push the
needle through the work and come up at
point C, take a small stitch and return to
the inside, pulling the thread tightly.
Repeat through points D and E. Come up
at point E again and fasten off.

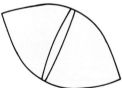
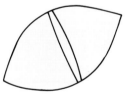

Trace the pattern for
the cat's features

Trace-off patterns for the Doorstop cat.

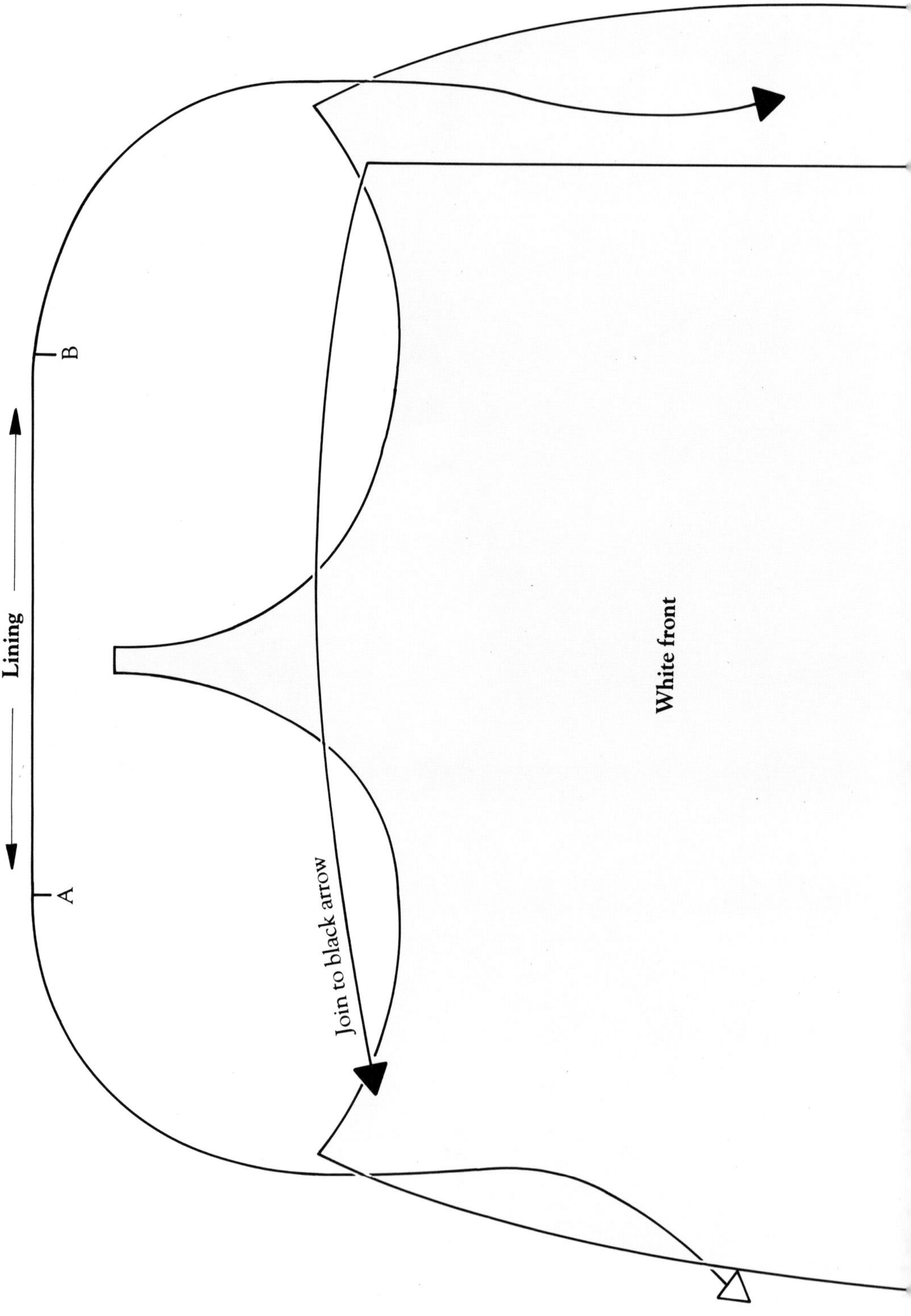

Lining

A

B

Join to black arrow

White front

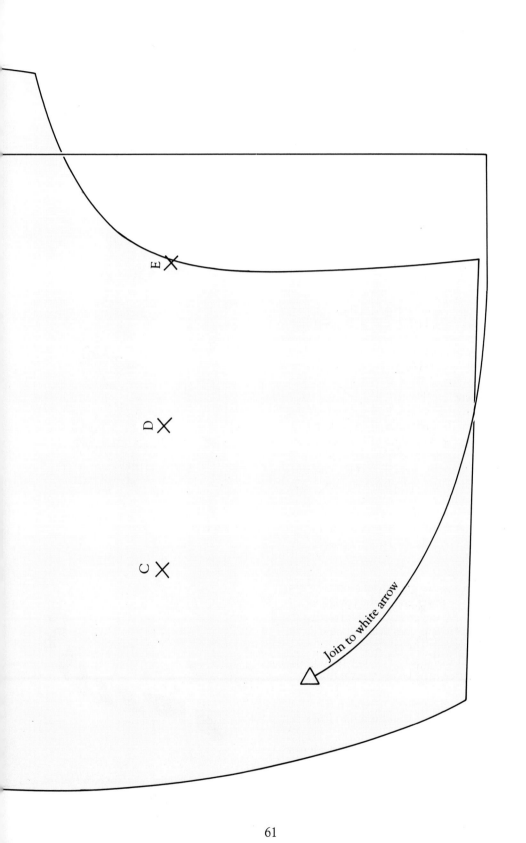

E ✕

D ✕

C ✕

Join to white arrow ◁

10 Snip the sides of the white jersey into random stripes, (refer to the picture) and glue or sew them in place.

11 Trace the cat's features. Retrace the pattern and cut out the eyes and nose. Cut two eyes from orange felt. Use the first tracing to position the felt shapes on the cat's face. Attach the eyes with running stitches. Work long, straight stitches across the eyes using black and white stranded thread. Embroider the nose and mouth with 6 strands of black stranded thread. Embroider the whiskers with straight stitches, using two strands of embroidery thread.

12 Work the division of the legs downwards from points C and D. Emphasize the body curve with point E in the centre with one or two rows of running stitches in black and white threads. Work along the curved lines below the eyes.

Finishing
13 Turn the cat upside down and remove the lid of the container. Fold back the fabric and wadding and fill the container with a mixture of pebbles and sand to weight it. Replace the lid firmly. Cut three 6in (15cm) strips of adhesive plaster and stick them across the lid and up the sides of the container under the wadding. Tie string tightly round the bottom of the container to hold the strips of plaster in place.

14 Run a gathering thread round the raw edge at the lower end of the cover fabric and draw up underneath the lid so that the container is now completely enclosed. Secure thread. The fabric should be stretched well down. You may need to trim the length a little before you do this.

15 Cut a circle of felt to neaten the bottom of the work and stitch in place.

16 For the tail, cut a piece of black jersey 13½ x 5in (34 x 12.5cm). With right sides facing, join the long edges and one short end, taking a ¼in (6mm) seam. Stuff the

tail lightly and close the open end. Cut a stripe of white jersey ¾in (18mm) wide and twist it diagonally round the tail and catch it in place. Work white running stitches along the edges of the stripe. Sew one end of the tail to the centre back and, with the seam next to the body, bring the tail round to the front. Catch in place.

Snip into the white jersey to form random stripes and glue or sew in place

Twist a white jersey stripe round the stuffed tail and catch in place with running stitches

Victorian lady

This little doll is made over a small bottle and makes a useful accessory for a dressing table or bureau.

Materials

A plastic bottle with a screw
   top about 6³/4in (17cm) tall
Flesh-coloured tights or stockings
Fabric for dress
Fabric for shawl (an old necktie is ideal)
Fabric for apron and petticoat
30in (75cm) of narrow lace
6in (15cm) square of black felt
Knitting wool for hair
Thin card
4 pipe cleaners
2 small black beads
Small wicker basket
Polyester toy filling
Scraps of narrow ribbon
Embroidery threads
Scrap of velvet fabric

Preparation

1 Weight the bottle by filling it with sand, and screw the top in place.

2 Cut a piece from the tights about 6in (15cm) long and tie one end in a knot. Insert sufficient stuffing into the knotted end so that when compressed firmly it forms a ball about 2¹/2in (6cm) diameter. Pull the open end over the bottle so that the screw top is buried in the stuffing. Stretch the tights downwards and tie the open end in a knot in front of the bottle base.

3 Cut and knot another piece of tights, then pull it over the first layer and knot at the bottle base so that there is now a double layer of fabric. Wind thread firmly round the bottle below the stuffing and secure.

MAKING THE DOLL
Needle-modelling the head

4 Insert a length of thread the same colour as the tights into a long needle and make a large knot at one end. Begin to model the head. (You may like to practise first on another prepared head.) If the results are not as you wish, just pull out the thread and start again. Push the needle into the top of the head and bring it out about a third of the way down the front, a little to

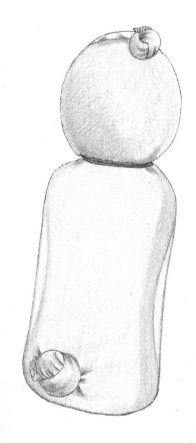

Pull the stuffed tube over the bottle and tie at the base. Knot and tie a second layer, then tie round for a neck

one side. Take a tiny stitch and push the needle back into the stuffing, then bring it out level with the first stitch but about ³/4in (18mm) away. Try to pick up plenty of stuffing and pull the thread to raise the bridge of the nose. Continue to take tiny stitches from side to side to raise the nose, then take small horizontal stitches to shape the nostrils. Sink the eye sockets by stitching from back to front of the head, and gathering slightly across the mouth.

5 Cut two eyes from white felt and glue them into the eye sockets, then stitch the black beads to the felt, taking the stitches from the back to the front of the head.

6 Embroider the eyebrows with 2 strands of dark grey thread and work small, straight stitches at the outer corner of the eyes for wrinkles.

7 Embroider the mouth with 2 strands of pink-brown thread. Colour the cheeks with tiny dots of lipstick and blend the dots smoothly with your finger.

8 Cut 5 strands of wool 12in (30cm) long, take them across the front of the head and tie at the back. Tie the ends together, twist and stitch the excess wool into in a small bun. Work a single straight stitch at the centre front for a parting.

Clothes
9 Cut a circle of petticoat fabric 10in (25cm) diameter. Run a gathering thread around the edges. Place the bottle centrally on the fabric circle, draw up the gathering thread to the waist of the bottle and fasten off.

10 For the skirt, cut a piece of fabric 13^1/$_2$ x 6in (34 x 15cm). With right sides facing, join the short ends taking a ^{1}/$_4$in (6mm) seam. Press the seam open. On one long edge, press ^{1}/$_4$in (6mm) to the wrong side, then turn a 1^1/$_2$in (4cm) hem to the wrong side and baste in place. This will be the depth of the pockets. Turn to the right side and turn up the hem so that its lower edge is now at the bottom of the fabric tube.

11 Stitch six evenly spaced vertical divisions around the hem to form separate pockets. Cut 20in (51cm) of narrow lace, join the short ends and catch in place under the skirt hem. Run a gathering thread round the upper edge, slip on to the doll and draw up to fit the waist.

12 Cut sufficient fabric to fit round the top of the bottle as a bodice. Join the short ends, right sides facing. Turn in the neck and waist edges ^{1}/$_4$in (6mm) and gather. Fit the bodice on to bottle, draw up the gathering threads and secure.

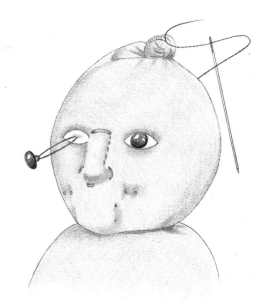

Glue white felt eyes into the sockets and then sew black beads to the middle, pulling the stitches through to the back of the head

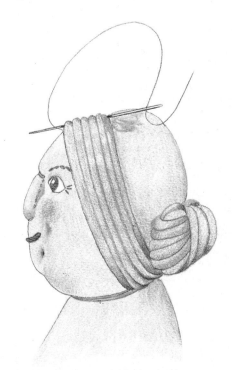

Tie strands of wool across the forehead and twist the ends into a bun at the back of the head

13 From the fine white fabric, cut an apron 4½ x 3¼in (11 x 8cm). Fold in half widthways with right sides facing. Stitch the two short sides taking a ¼in (6mm) seam. Turn to right side. Gather up the raw edges and catch the apron to the centre waist. Tie on a ribbon waistband.

Arms and hands

14 Twist a pipe cleaner to make the lower arm and hand shape. Twist another pipe cleaner into the first to extend the arm and hand to 3¼in (8cm). Pull a small piece of doubled tights fabric over the hand. Needle-model and embroider the fingers and nails. Cover the arm with a tube of fabric cut on the bias. Sew the top of the sleeve neatly on to the shoulder. Make and cover another arm in the same way.

Finishing

15 Cut a thin piece of card for the bonnet brim 5½ x 1in (14 x 2.5cm), round off the corners of one long edge. Cover both sides with a folded piece of black felt. Oversew all the edges. For the bonnet crown, cut a piece of black felt 8 x 2in (20 x 5cm) and gather one long edge. Oversew from the wrong side to one long edge of the brim, then gather the remaining edge tightly for the centre back. Gather the remaining narrow lace and catch under the front of the bonnet brim then catch the bonnet to the head with a few stitches. Sew ribbon ties to the lower edge of the brim and tie in a bow under the chin.

16 For the shawl, cut a triangle of fabric on the bias 10 x 4in (25 x 10cm). (You may need to join pieces if you are using an old necktie.) Neaten the edges and place round the doll's shoulders, catch in place with a few stitches.

17 Cut an oval of velvet for the top of the basket and gather the edges. Pull up the gathers, push a small ball of toy filling and push into the basket. Slip the handle of the basket over the doll's arm, and catch the hand to the waistband of the apron with a few stitches.

Twist pipe cleaners to make the hand and arm, shaping the hand as you work

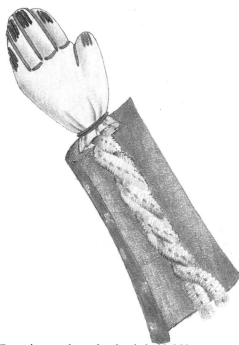

Cover the pipe cleaner hand with doubled fabric and needle-model the fingers and nails

THREE

Little Dolls

Christmas fairies

Make a flight of tiny fairies for the Christmas tree or hang a single fairy at each window pane.

Materials
For one fairy:
1 pipe cleaner
Scrap of pink tights fabric
3/4in (18mm)-diameter paper bead
Adhesive
Scrap of gold Lurex jersey fabric
Gold Lurex thread
4in (10cm) piece of 3/8in (9mm)-wide
    white ribbon
4in (10cm) piece of 1 3/4in (4.5cm)-
    wide broderie anglaise
Small piece of transparent film (from a gift
    box lid)
Fine gold marker pen
Fine felt-tipped pens
Tiny artificial flowers

Making the doll

1 For the arms, cut a 2in (5cm) piece of pipe cleaner and roll it in a small strip cut from the tights fabric. Secure with a few stitches at each end. Fold the remaining cleaner in half, brush a little glue on the ends and push them into the paper bead. Leave to dry, then cover the bead with a doubled layer of of tights fabric. Gather the excess fabric under the head and tie round tightly with matching thread.

2 For the hair, cut a 6in (15cm) strip of gold jersey on the bias, 1/4in (6mm) wide. Touch glue to the top of the head and press the end of the fabric on to the glue. Wind the fabric round the head to cover it (see picture). Finish the end in a small knot on top of the head and secure with a few stitches. Wind gold thread round to shape the topknot.

3 Mark in the face with a felt-tipped pen (follow the picture).

Cross the white ribbon over the body and upper arms. Tie the waist to secure the ribbon

Draw the veins on the wings with gold pen, then fold and sew to the fairy's back

Fairy mobile
These pretty little dolls would be ideal for making a Christmas wreath mobile on a florist's foam ring. Push sprays of silvered greenery or white and silver plastic foliage into the ring to cover it. Suspend the ring on silver and green ribbons. Tie the fairies to transparent nylon thread and suspend them from the ring, spacing them equidistantly. The fairies could also be made in red and gold or in blue and silver.

4 Fold the prepared arms piece in half and catch to the body just under the head. Cut the white ribbon in two and cross each piece over the body and upper arms. Wind thread around the waist to secure the ribbon.

Finishing
5 Join the short ends of the broderie anglaise and gather the straight edges to fit around the fairy's waist. Slip on and catch in place with a few stitches. Wind gold thread around the waist and tie off.

6 Trace the pattern for the wings on paper. Cut out and place on the clear film. Draw round with the gold marker pen. Then mark in the veins. Cut out, fold on the dotted lines and catch to the centre back of the fairy.

7 Wind thread round a bunch of the tiny flowers and catch them in between the top of the arms. Add a bow of very narrow ribbon. Attach a short length of gold thread to the fairy's topknot and the other end to the edge of her skirt.

House of dolls

This tiny house contains a family of seven dolls, complete with a cat.
The features of the dolls are formed using a
needle-modelling technique.

Materials

For each doll

3in (7.5cm) piece of doubled fabric cut from the leg of tights or stocking

6 x 3in (15 x 7.5cm) bias-cut piece of fabric for the body

Double knitting wool for hair (see pictures for colours)

Stranded embroidery threads

Narrow ribbon, lace and trimmings

Polyester toy filling

For the house

2 pieces of 17³/4 x 14¹/4in (45 x 36cm) of craft-weight Vilene (Pellon)

19³/4 x 15³/4in (50 x 40cm) piece of fabric for the interior

10 x 8in (25 x 20cm) piece of fabric for the roof

15¹/4 x 12¹/2in (39 x 32cm) piece of fabric for the exterior

Felt scraps for trimmings

Large press fastener

Making the basic doll

1 Head: Put a small ball of stuffing in the centre of the tights fabric and bring the raw edges together so that the stuffing is firmly compressed to the size of a walnut. Wind sewing thread round under the ball and secure, leave the excess fabric projecting.

2 Body: With right sides together, fold the body fabric in half across the width and join the short edges taking a ¹/4in (6mm) seam. Re-fold so that the seam runs down the centre back. Stitch across one end and pull up the thread as much as possible to gather. Turn to the right side. Stuff the body firmly then turn a ¹/4in (6mm) hem to the wrong side at the top of the body and gather. Insert the surplus fabric of the head into the body and draw up the gathering thread. Stitch the head to the body at the neck.

3 Face: This is needle-modelled. To do this, push the needle through the fabric and stuffing and pull up the thread to create the features. A face will emerge as you sew. Start with a knot on the end of

Stuff doubled fabric for the head and tie to secure.

Make the body tube, gather the bottom, stuff and then gather and insert the head

Character dolls like these would make ideal items for bazaars and fund-raising. They could be made to look like well-known figures, such as pop stars.

the thread and insert the needle through the back of the neck to the centre front. Make a round nose by stitching in a circle, then draw up the thread, back stitch to secure. (Other noses are made with straight stitches.) Sink eyes and shape ears by stitching through the head. Embroider the features using French knots and straight stitches for the eyes and stem stitch for the mouths. Colour the cheeks with tiny dots of lipstick, then smudge them with a tissue.

4 Measure over the head to find the total length of the hair, then wind yarn round your fingers or a piece of card cut to this measurement. Tie round the middle of the bunch of wool and stitch to the top of the head. Catch the lower ends of the wool strands to the head.

5 **Arms:** Cut a strip of pink or beige felt $3^1/2$ x $^3/8$in (9cm x 9mm). Turn and sew a $^3/8$in (9mm) hem on the short ends of the strip for hands. Cut a piece of fabric 2in (5cm) square. Place the felt centrally on the wrong side of the fabric, roll the fabric round the felt. Pin in place. Cut the piece in two halves. Sew the overlapped fabric in place. Catch the ends of the arms to either side of body just below the neck.

INDIVIDUAL DOLLS
Mother
6 Stitch ric-rac braid to the body (see picture) and add a bead to the centre neck for a brooch. Cut a circle of felt $3^1/4$ x $2^1/4$in (8 x 6cm) for the hat, gather lightly $^5/8$in (15mm) from the edge. Position the hat on the head, secure the gathering thread and stitch the hat in place, inserting a little stuffing under the crown. Sew on an artificial flower.

Father
7 For the body, cut 2 pieces of fabric, one for the shirt and one for the trousers. Seam them together, right sides facing, before trimming to size. Embroider the spectacles on the face and add a felt necktie.

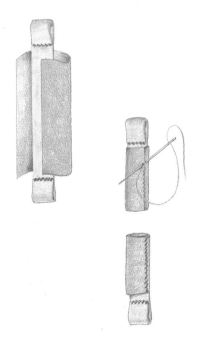

Roll the fabric round the felt, cut into two arms and sew to secure the overlap

More ideas for little toys
The method used to make the family of dolls and their cat could be adapted to make other groups of figures and animals. A Noah's ark of animals with Noah, Mrs Noah and Ham, Shem and Japhet would be one variation. Choose fabrics with suitable patterns for the animals, such as stripes for tigers and zebras, spots for leopards, grey velour for elephants and reddish velour for lions and monkeys. Each of the human figures could have a white fabric head covering and the male figures could have black, knitting yarn beards. The little house could also be adapted to an ark. Cover a small shoe box with fabric inside and outside and cut circles of felt for portholes. Glue them along the sides. Glue a smaller box inside for the deck and glue the little doll's house to the deck.

Granny

8 For the knitted shawl, cast on 2 stitches using 4 ply knitting wool and size 11 knitting needles. Work every row in knit stitches. Increase 1 stitch at the beginning of every row until the work measures 1½in (4cm) across. Work 3 rows straight, then decrease 1 stitch on the same edge on every other row until 2 stitches remain, cast off. Sew the shawl round Granny's shoulders. Add an apron made from a scrap of lace.

Grandpa

9 Make the body as for Father. For his pullover back, cast on 12 stitches, using 4 ply knitting wool and size 11 knitting needles. Work every row in knit stiches.

Continue straight until the work measures ³/4in (18mm). Cast off 2 stitches at the beginning of the next two 2 rows, continue straight for desired length to shoulder, cast off. Knit the front in the same way, but when the armhole shapings are complete, knit 2 stitches together in the centre of the next row, and complete each side separately. Decrease 1 stitch at the neck edge on following alternate rows, work straight until the back matches the front. Cast off. Complete the other side front in the same way. Join the sides seams and one shoulder on the wrong side, slip on to doll, join the other shoulder.

10 Embroider spectacles in gold thread. Refer to the diagram on page 85.

78

Big sister

11 Embroider loops of knitting yarn at the front of the hair for a fringe, add tiny bows to either side of the head. Cut a strip of fabric for the skirt 8 x 1$^{1}/4$in (20 x 3cm), neaten one long edge and gather the other. Sew round the centre of the body. Sew narrow braid at the waist and neck.

Little brother

12 Make the body as for the Father. For the cap, cut 2 triangles each of red and white felt measuring $^{3}/4$in (18mm) at the base and with $^{5}/8$in (15mm) sides. Join the triangles with oversewing on the edges to make a circle of alternating colours. Cut a peak to the cap from felt and sew to the crown. Stitch the cap to the head, inserting some stuffing under it. Using doubled knitting yarn, work French knots for curls over the head. Make braces (suspenders) for the trousers from ribbon. Sew on beads for buttons. Tie a ribbon scarf round the doll's neck.

Baby

13 Make the baby's head and body a little smaller than the other dolls, and use piece of the same colour tights fabric for the body. Make the arms from a small piece of rolled-up tights fabric. Make the bonnet from a 3in (7.5cm) piece of 1¼in (3cm)-wide lace. Gather on one long edge, draw up and stitch to the centre back of the head. Gather again about ³/₈in (9mm) away from other long edge, draw up to encircle the face. Work French knots of knitting yarn for the hair. For the robe, cut a piece of lace or broderie anglaise 6 x 3¼in (15 x 8cm). With right sides together, join the short edges with a ¼in (6mm) seam. Gather the straight edge, slip on to the doll, snip armholes, draw up gathering thread and secure to the neck. Sew a tiny ribbon bow to the centre front.

Cat

14 Cut and join the edges of a piece of jersey fabric (as for dolls' bodies) and stuff. Gather the top edge and draw up to close the opening. Run another gathering thread round 1in (2.5cm) below the top of the body, draw up a little and secure to shape the neck. Needle-model the face and embroider features (see picture). For each ear, cut a ⁵/₈in (15mm) square of fabric, fold diagonally and stitch in place. Take a long stitch down the centre front of the cat to suggest the division of front legs. For the tail, roll a tube of fabric, sew the raw edge, sew to the cat. Sew on a ribbon bow.

MAKING THE HOUSE

15 Following the diagram on page 83, draw a pattern for the house on stiff paper, and mark in the dotted lines. Cut the shape twice from craft-weight Vilene (Pellon). Glue the two layers together with a few dabs of adhesive. Mark the dotted lines shown on the paper pattern on one layer only. Lay the fabric for the lining wrong side facing and place the interfacing on top, allowing the surplus fabric evenly all round. Fold the surplus fabric over the edges A-B, D-E, F-G and H-I. Press in place and pin.

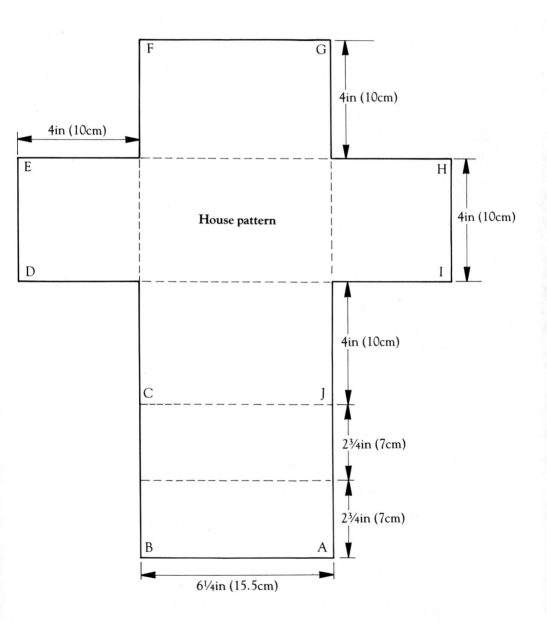

16 With the interfacing layer uppermost, machine straight stitch across the fold on A-B within 1/4in (6mm) of the edge. Re-set the machine to an open zigzag stitch approximately 1/4in (6mm) wide, and stitch from B-C-D so that on the right of the stitch, the needle encloses the edge of the interfacing. Continue to stitch all round in the same way. Trim away the surplus fabric as close to the zigzag stitching as possible. Stitch across all dotted lines marked on the interfacing, sewing through interfacing and lining.

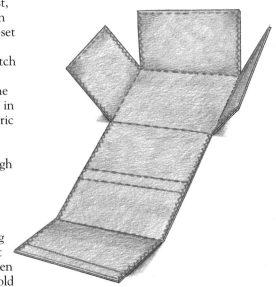

Trim away the surplus fabric, stitch across all marked dotted lines

Exterior

17 Place the exterior fabric wrong side uppermost. Position the interfaced lining on top with the lining uppermost so that the surplus exterior fabric all round is even and the edge extends just beyond J-C. Fold in the surplus along three edges D-E, so that the surplus fabric is underneath the right side of exterior fabric. Press in place and pin.

18 Stitch with zigzag stitches from C-D. Re-set the machine to straight stitch and stitch across the folded edges D-I. Continue in this way all round. Trim the surplus fabric outside the zigzag stitches.

Handle and roof

19 Cut a strip of roof fabric for the handle 8 x 2in (20 x 5cm). Fold along the length

Baste the handle ends 2in (5cm) apart

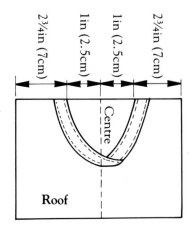

2³/4in (7cm) 1in (2.5cm) 1in (2.5cm) 2³/4in (7cm)

Centre

Roof

with right sides together, join with a 1/4in (6mm) seam. Turn to the right side. Press, so that the seam runs down the centre of the strip. Top stitch close to the long edges.

20 Fold the roof fabric in half across the width and cut to give two pieces each 7¹/2 x 4³/4in (19 x 12cm). Baste the raw edges of the handle to the right side of one piece, placing them centrally 2in (5cm) apart. With right sides together, place the other roof piece on top, join, enclosing the handle edges within 5/8in (15mm) of the edge. Turn to the right side, press the seam allowance open.

21 With wrong sides facing, pin the roof to the outside of the house, placing the seam over J-C. Fold all the surplus fabric to the inside so that folds are level with the three edges J-A-B-B and the roof overlaps the exterior fabric by 3/4in (18mm) beyond the edge J-C. Press the folds and pin. Top stitch the roof all round close to the edge. Top stitch either side of the centre roof seam in the same way.

Decoration

22 Cut door and windows from felt, embroider as desired (see picture), and then sew to the outside of house front. Surround the door with felt roses and leaves, attaching them with straight stitches and French knots.

MAKING THE HOUSE

23 With the lining side of the house facing, fold it so that the short edges from the corners E and F are together. Pin and then join with straight machine-stitching. Join all the other edges on the front, sides and back of the house. Turn to the right side. Sew half of the press fastener to the centre front of the roof on the inside. Sew the other half on the corresponding edge of the outside front.

Tiny doll families that are small enough to fit into a doll's house are sometimes difficult to find in toy departments. If the dolls in this chapter are too large, try making them from pipe cleaners and velvet ribbon tubing, with paper ball heads. Cut pieces of velvet tubing for the body, legs and arms and push pieces of pipe cleaner inside. Glue wooden beads on the ends of the arms and legs. Glue the body together. Dress the doll in felt and, when it is completely dressed, glue a pink-painted paper ball on for a head. Make the doll's hair with knitting yarn, glueing it round the paper bead. Mark in the features with a felt-tipped pen. If you would like the dolls to stand up, cut an oval from stiff card and cover it with felt. Omit the bead feet and glue the doll's pipe cleaner legs to the card.

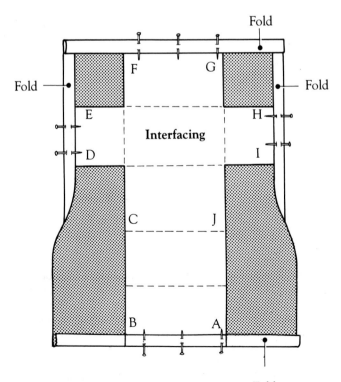

Pin the roof to the outside of the house

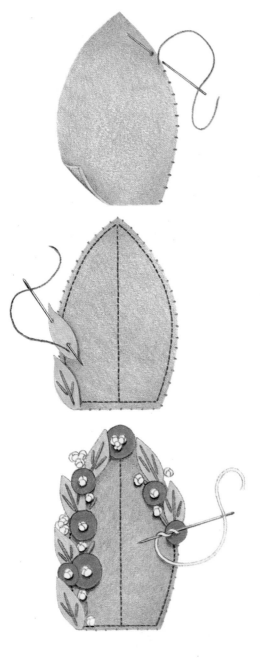

Little brother: Work French knots for curls over the head

Granny: Sew the wool loops to the head

Twist the ends on top of the head and sew

Cut felt roses and leaves, then attach them round the door with straight stitches and French knots

Big sister: Embroider loops of knitting yarn for a front fringe

Father: Embroider the spectacles on the doll's face

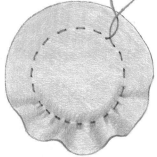

Mother: Gather a felt circle ³/₈in (9mm) from the edge

Grandfather: Embroider the doll's spectacles in gold thread

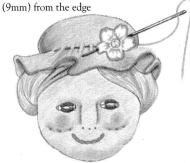

Sew the hat to the head adding a flower

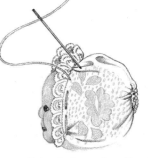

Baby: Gather up ³/₈in (9mm) from the fabric edge to encircle the face

Cat: Embroider the cat's features

Fold fabric squares for ears, sew to the head

Dolly pocket

This small, novelty doll is worn round the neck on a ribbon and makes a very pretty and unusual purse.

Materials

Small pieces of gingham and white cotton fabrics
Small pieces of jersey fabrics
4 ply knitting wool for hair
Stranded embroidery threads
2 sequins (or felt) for eyes
32in (80cm) of 1/8in (3mm)-wide ribbon
3in (7.5cm) of narrow elastic
51/2in (14cm) of narrow, decorative trimming
Small button

Preparation

1 Draw the patterns from the diagrams. Seam allowances of 1/4in (6mm) are included.

2 From white cotton, cut two head pieces, eight hand pieces, eight feet pieces.

3 From gingham, cut two back bodies. For the front body, cut the pattern along the dotted line A-B and add 1/4in (6mm) to the upper straight edge. Cut one front body from gingham. Cut one apron pocket and a 9in (23cm)-diameter circle from white fabric for a hat.

Making the doll

4 With right sides facing, stitch all round the head leaving a gap for turning. Turn to the right side and stuff. Close the opening. Sew on the eye sequins (or cut circles from felt) and sew to the face with three long, straight stitches (see picture). Embroider a curved mouth in stem stitch. Dot lipstick on the cheeks and blend the dots with a finger tip.

5 Press 1/4in (6mm) to the wrong side of the apron pocket and stitch across. Baste the pocket to the centre of the front body.

Stitch round the curved edge and top stitch trimming round the curve. Sew the button to the top centre of the pocket.

6 Press 1/4in (6mm) to the wrong side along the upper edge of the body front. On the wrong side, pin and baste the elastic to the ends of the pressed edge. Stretch the elastic to fit and top stitch.

7 With right sides facing, place the hands and feet together in pairs and stitch round the curved edges. Turn to the right side and press. With the corresponding edges together, and right sides facing, baste the front body on top of a back body piece, stretching the elastic. Place the hands and feet as shown in the picture on page 87 and, with right sides facing, pin the other back body on top. Stitch the seam, leaving the edge C-D open. Turn to the right side and press.

8 With right sides facing, baste C-D on the body, halfway up the back head. Sew by hand.

Finishing

9 To make the hair, wind knitting yarn round two fingers several times. Slip from the fingers and tie yarn round the middle of the bunch, leaving a long end. Stitch the hair to the head, placing three bunches on the centre of the head and two at each side.

10 Neaten the edge of the hat fabric, then gather within 1in (2.5cm) of the edge. Draw up to fit the head. Stitch the hat to the head firmly. Sew ribbon to the top of the head with the ends about 11/2in (4cm) apart.

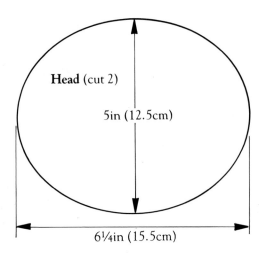

Head (cut 2)

5in (12.5cm)

6¼in (15.5cm)

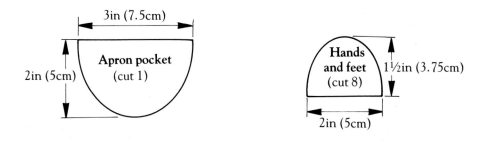

3in (7.5cm)

Apron pocket
(cut 1)

2in (5cm)

**Hands
and feet**
(cut 8)

1½in (3.75cm)

2in (5cm)

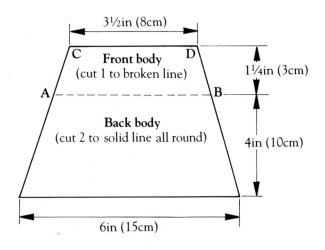

3½in (8cm)

C   **Front body**   D
(cut 1 to broken line)

1¼in (3cm)

A — — — — — — — — B

Back body
(cut 2 to solid line all round)

4in (10cm)

6in (15cm)

Baby bunting

This tiny doll in a cradle is very simple to make and could be completed in just an hour or two.

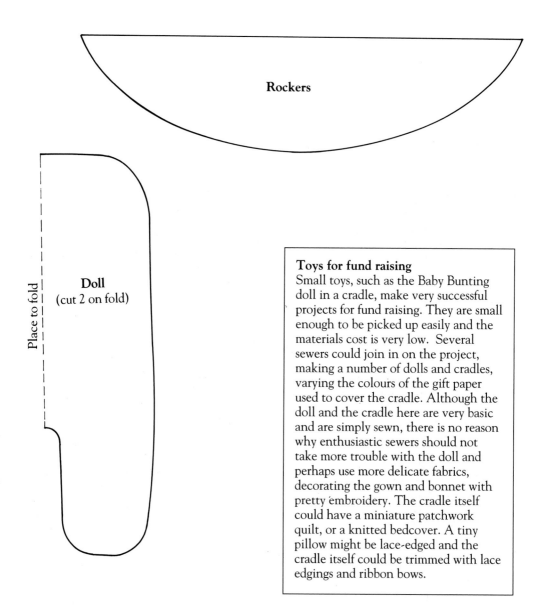

Rockers

Doll
(cut 2 on fold)

Place to fold

Toys for fund raising
Small toys, such as the Baby Bunting doll in a cradle, make very successful projects for fund raising. They are small enough to be picked up easily and the materials cost is very low. Several sewers could join in on the project, making a number of dolls and cradles, varying the colours of the gift paper used to cover the cradle. Although the doll and the cradle here are very basic and are simply sewn, there is no reason why enthusiastic sewers should not take more trouble with the doll and perhaps use more delicate fabrics, decorating the gown and bonnet with pretty embroidery. The cradle itself could have a miniature patchwork quilt, or a knitted bedcover. A tiny pillow might be lace-edged and the cradle itself could be trimmed with lace edgings and ribbon bows.

Materials
Cylindrical salt container
Gift paper (for covering container)
Fabric scraps for the doll's body and for the bedclothes
Polyester toy filling (for mattress)
Stranded embroidery threads
Felt-tipped pens
Thin card
Adhesive
9in (23cm) of 1¹/₂in (4cm)-wide broderie anglaise edging

Preparation
1 Cut the top from the salt container and replace it with a piece of card cut to the same shape. Tape in place. Cut a section away from the container. Cover the outside and the inside of both ends with the gift paper.

MAKING THE CRADLE
2 Neaten the straight sides of the cradle with two strips of card. Glue them in place

3 Cut slots for the rockers, ³/₄in (18mm) from the cradle ends. Trace the rockers pattern and cut from card. Cover them with gift paper. Glue the rockers into the slots.

4 For a pillow, cut two 3in (7.5cm) squares of cotton fabric, place together right sides facing and stitch on three sides. Turn right side out, stuff and close the open end.

5 For a mattress, cut two rectangles of fabric 6 x 4in (15 x 10cm). Place together right sides facing and stitch on three sides. Turn right side out, stuff and close the open end. Cut a blanket from fleecy fabric, using pinking shears.

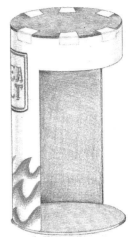

Tape card top into salt container. Cut out a section, cover inside ends and outside with gift paper

MAKING THE DOLL

6 Trace the pattern for the doll and cut out. Cut the shape from white or pink fabric and cut out a front and back. With right sides together, stitch all round, taking a ¹/₄in (6mm) seam and leaving a gap in the seam for turning and the leg ends open.

7 Turn right side out and stuff. Oversew the leg ends to close.

8 For one arm, cut a piece of fabric 1¹/₂in (4cm) square. With right sides facing, fold in half and join the two edges together, then stitch across the end, rounding the end for a hand. Turn to the right side and stuff. Close the open end and stitch the arm to the side of the body. Make another arm in the same way and attach to the other side of the body.

Cut slots in the underside, cover rocker shapes with paper and glue into the slots

9 For hair, wind embroidery thread round two fingers and slip the loops off. Catch the loops down the middle to the front of the head. Indicate the doll's face with felt-tipped pen.

10 If you prefer, embroider the doll's face with stranded embroidery threads. Work the eyes in tiny stem stiches, so that they look closed and the mouth in chain stitch.

11 Make the nightdress from 6in (15cm) of broderie anglaise trimming, gathered along the straight edge. Cut slots for arms. Slip on to the doll and catch the edges together at the centre back. Gather the remainder of the broderie anglaise and catch to the head for a bonnet. The doll can wear a small triangle of fleecy fabric for a nappy.

Baby doll

This tiny doll will be very popular with small girls. Older children could probably make it themselves, with a little help from an adult.

Materials
Child's ankle sock (or knee sock)
Knitting wool (for the pompon)
Polyester toy filling
Short piece of narrow ribbon
Stranded embroidery threads in pink and
  pale blue
A little lipstick

Preparation
1 Cut off the leg or ankle part of the sock, about 2in (5cm) above the heel.

MAKING THE DOLL
2 Stuff the toe and run a gathering thread about one-third down the foot, to form the head.

3 Fold the rest of the leg flat and cut a slit up the centre about 2in (5cm) long. Stuff the remainder of the body, pushing stuffing into the heel so that the doll will sit up.

4 To form the legs, join the sides of the slit and the remainder of the cut edge, taking the raw edge to the inside, stuffing as you sew. Gather the leg ends.

5 For the arms and the cap, cut the remainder of the sock. With right sides facing, join each of the two smaller pieces on one short and the long sides. Turn to the right side, stuff lightly and gather the remaining open ends slightly and stitch them to the body for the arms.

6 Gather the cut edge of the remaining piece on the wrong side for a cap and pull over the head.

7 Make a small pompon from yarn and sew it to the top of the cap. Embroider the features (see picture), working the eyes in

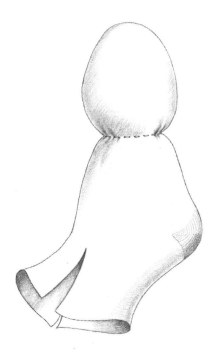

Stuff the sock toe for a head and gather about one-third down. Cut a 2in (5cm) slit up the centre

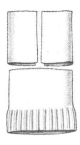

Cut the remainder of the sock for the arms and cap

straight stitches and the mouth in stem stitch. Dot a little lipstick on the cheeks and blend it with a finger tip.

Flying witch

You could make several of these amusing dolls for Hallowe'en decorations.

Materials
Tights or stockings in brown or beige
8in (20cm) square of black felt
6 x 8³/4in (15 x 22cm) piece of black
  fabric
2 black beads
10in (25cm) piece of stick
Small dried twigs
2 pipe cleaners

Making the witch
1 Cut a 12in (30cm) piece from the tights.
Stuff lightly then bring the cut ends
together and knot at the front of the body.

2 Using matching thread, take long
stitches through the body to shape the
face, pulling the stitches tightly. Stitch on
beads for eyes.

3 **Legs:** Lay 2 pipe cleaners together and
twist them loosely. Bend in half, bend up
the ends for feet. Bind the legs with narrow
strips cut from the tights fabric. Cut 4 felt
shapes and sew to make boots. Sew on to
the legs. Sew the legs to the front of the
body, over the knot.

4 Round off two corners of the black fabric
square, then wrap the cloak round the
witch. Sew the front edges together.

5 Make the broomstick by binding twigs
round the stick with wire. Sew the
broomstick to the front of the witch.

6 For the hat, draw a circle 2¹/2in (6cm)
diameter on paper. Cut one quarter out.
Use as a pattern to cut the shape from felt.
Draw a 4in (10cm)-diameter circle and
another circle inside ³/4in (18mm) in
diameter. Cut out for a pattern and cut
from felt. Sew the crown of the hat
together and then sew into the brim. Glue
the hat to the head.

Make the witch's hat from a cone of black felt
and sew it into a black felt ring

Hallowe'en witchery
Amusing witch dolls could be the focal
point of a hallowe'en party decorations.
Make several and tie them to the edges
of a hanging lamp shade. Hang them
from wires so that they are suspended at
different heights over the party table.
They could also be fastened to a wall
with double-sided sticky tape, perhaps
two or three of them in a witch flight.

FOUR

Better Doll Making

❦

*Everything you need to know to be successful in doll making
is in this chapter. When things go wrong, it is usually because you are
working too quickly, trying to take a short cut - or using
materials other than those recommended.
Here's how to avoid the pitfalls.*

BASIC TOOLS AND EQUIPMENT

Toymakers starting on their first doll are usually delighted to find that they already have most of the equipment they need in their sewing box, especially if they do dressmaking or home sewing. The checklist overleaf will show you the various items you need.

A sewing machine is useful for doll making but not essential. Machine-stitching saves time and looks neat and a zigzag facility is useful for neatening seams or working on jersey fabrics. However, neat hand sewing can be just as strong and hardwearing and a hand-made doll has a special charm all of its own. You will need an iron and ironing board. Pressing seams as you go along not only makes for a better finish but it is important where a second line of stitching crosses a previous join, such as when sewing together the inner leg seams of trousers. Plan a special corner where you can leave your unfinished doll undisturbed. You will need a table or work top for cutting out out fabric and, of course, a good working light - essential when sewing in small scale.

Scissors

You will need at least three pairs of scissors. First, dressmaking scissors with sharp blades and pointed tips are required for cutting out fabrics. A small pair of pointed embroidery scissors is useful for trimming seams, snipping into seam allowances and for cutting thread. Finally, find an old pair of scissors and keep them for cutting out card and paper. (If you think you are likely to confuse your paper scissors with the cutting out pair, tie a piece of bright thread to the handle of one pair, so that you can quickly see which is which.)

Pinking shears are useful for cutting out felt decoratively and for trimming seam allowances.

Pins

When making toys, it is a good idea to use as few pins as possible in case one gets lost inside the doll and becomes a source of danger later. Choose glass-headed dressmaker's pins because these are easy to see on your work table (and on the floor) and there is less likelihood of their becoming misplaced. Count them as you use them in the fabric and again when they are removed to make sure that none are left in the doll. Always put pins back in their box or stick them into a pincushion.

Needles

The size of needle used for hand-sewing is often a personal preference but generally, medium-sized needles are best for general sewing while short, long-eyed crewel needles are used for embroidery. A long darning needle is useful for working with wool yarn (such as making doll's hair styles). A bodkin is needed for threading elastic through casings or ribbon through eyelet lace.

Cottage sewing box
The house pattern on page 83 would make a very pretty and unusual sewing box as a gift for a little girl. Increase all the measurements of the house pattern by 50%. Cut the shape from fabric, as · instructed then iron the fabric on to medium-weight iron-on interfacing. Cut pieces of card to the size and shape of each section, 4 walls, the bottom and two roof pieces. Glue the card to the interfacing side of the house. Cut and work the lining as described and sew or glue to the house outer. This will make a structure that is firmer. Sew small pockets on the inside of the house and glue a piece of felt to the inside of the roof for pins and needles.

Stuffing tools
Usually, doll's heads, bodies, legs and arms can be stuffed by hand, using your fingers but there will be small places where a special tool is required, to push the stuffing into place. Blunt pencils, knitting needles or even the scissor points can be used but if you are doing a lot of toymaking, it is good idea to make yourself a special stuffing tool. You need a short length of 1/4inin (6mm)-diameter wood dowelling - about 12in (30cm) will be sufficient. Shape one end to a blunt point, using first your craft knife then sandpaper the end until the point is smooth.

Pencils and pens
Pencils are needed for drawing out patterns and for tracing patterns over carbon paper. A dressmaker's chalk pencil is invaluable for transferring marks from pattern to fabric and for marking seam allowance lines. Felt-tipped pens in a selection of colours are useful for marking symbols and letters on patterns and are sometimes used for indicating features on character dolls.

Measuring aids
A tape measure is essential and you will also need a ruler for drawing out diagram patterns and as a straight edge when cutting paper and card. You will see that all the measurements in this book are given first in imperial (inches and yards) and then in metric (millimetres, centimentres and metres). Use either imperial or metric measurements but do not compare the two because they may not work out exactly the same. Where measurements are critical, an almost exact conversion is given but this is a rare occurrence.

Paper and card
Tracing paper is usually recommended for tracing same-size patterns but ordinary kitchen greaseproof paper will do just as well. Dressmaker's squared pattern paper, which is available in different scales, is used for enlarging graph patterns. Always check the scale of your pattern before purchasing the paper. Thin card is often recommended for making templates. The backs and fronts of cardboard cereal

packets will do quite well for this. You will sometimes need stiff card for cutting the formers required when winding wool yarn for doll's hair. Self-adhesive address labels are useful for sticking to felt when cutting out intricate shapes or small pieces.

Adhesives
The type of glue you use in doll making is important. When a clear, all-purpose glue is recommended for sticking card or paper, or for sticking down pieces of felt, choose one such as UHU. This dries quickly and the long, thin nozzle of the tube makes it easy to apply a tiny dot exactly where it is needed. (If this type of glue accidentally gets on to fabric, remove it with acetone but remember that acetone is volatile and inflammable so work in a well-ventilated place.)

Latex adhesive (white from the tube or jar and dries clear) will stick fabric together or to paper and card.

THREADS, YARNS AND FABRICS
It is a basic rule of sewing that the thread should match the fabric not only in colour, but in the fibre. Use an all-purpose synthetic thread (such as Drima) when sewing fabrics of man-made fibres. This is a cotton-covered polyester thread that combines strength with a good appearance and it is suitable for most types of fabric. The colour range is extensive and you can use this thread for most modern fabrics. Soft cotton thread is suitable for basting and for fabrics made of pure cotton.

Six-stranded embroidery cotton is used for embroidery. All six strands are worked together where a solid effect is required (perhaps for an eye or for a nose). For features such as eyelashes and mouths or for general decorative stitchery, two or three strands together are sufficient. There are several brands available in shops and the colour ranges are extensive.

Wool yarn
Knitting wool is often recommended for making doll's hair and the best kinds are double knitting and chunky wools. The quality need not be good – acrylic or nylon/wool mixtures are adequate. Small amounts are needed for a head of hair and you will usually find that a 25g ball is sufficient. If you are making dolls regularly, it is worth buying odd balls of knitting wool in sales as these are usually cheaper. Brown, black, yellow, cream, red and grey are the colours you will be using mostly.

ENGLISH/AMERICAN GLOSSARY

English	American
Bias binding	Bias strip
Buttonhole thread	Buttonhole twist
Copydex adhesive	Slomans latex adhesive
Cotton wool	Surgical cotton
Elastic bands	Rubber bands
Hardboard	Fibreboard
Iron-on interfacing	Non-woven fusible interfacing
Muslin	Cheesecloth
Polyester wadding	Polyester batting
Sellotape	Scotchtape
Stockinette	Cotton-knit fabric
Tack	Baste
Velvet	Silky napped fabric
(In knitting)	
Cast off	Bind off

Choosing fabrics

The pattern instructions in this book recommend the type of fabric you should use for the project. Generally, choose firm, closely-woven fabrics rather than loose weaves which fray more easily when narrow seams are being worked. If you are particularly keen to use a soft, loose-weave fabric (such as for a doll's party dress), paint the cut edges with a fray-inhibiting liquid before sewing. Alternatively, back the fabric with light-weight iron-on interfacing.

Re-using fabrics

Part of the fun in doll making comes from using up bits of fabric left over from sewing projects. Often, quite small pieces are needed for doll's garments and it is worth saving every scrap that comes your way. Ask dressmaking friends for left-over pieces and start a ragbag of oddments. Sometimes, bazaars or jumble sales have outgrown children's clothing for sale. Look these over carefully and see if parts less worn can be cut away and re-used. Wash fabrics thoroughly, discard the worn bits and iron the remaining scraps smooth, ready for your next doll-making project.

Search sales counters for small, end-of-roll lengths of expensive fabrics – and buy them for a few pence.

When choosing colours for doll's clothes, colour, texture and pattern are enormously important to a child. Fine or lightweight fabrics in clear tones and bright primaries, in plains or small-scale prints, should be your first choice. Avoid heavily embroidered fabrics, brocades, richly ornamented laces, thick, shiny satins and ribbed silks. Colourful organzas, gauzes, metallic-threaded nylons are acceptable for doll's party wear, or for character dolls where colour and glitter are part of the costume. Fabrics for doll making (opposite) provides some useful guidance.

Buying by mail order

There are a number of mail order suppliers of fabrics and addresses can be found in crafts magazines. These suppliers usually sell bags of assorted pieces quite cheaply,

and, occasionally, can provide you with polyester toy filling and felt as well. It is recommended that, whenever possible you purchase good quality felt. Some types pull apart easily and feel rather rough on the surface. The better qualities are soft and flexible and evenly coloured.

Interfacings

Non-woven interfacings are very useful in doll making. Generally sold under the brand name of Vilene (Pellon in the USA), interfacings come in different weights, in white, grey and black.

Iron-on interfacings are useful for backing thin fabrics and felt and can be used to back stockinette when this fabric is being used for doll's bodies. A backing of a light interfacing can help to control the stretch of knitted fabrics and this can be a help when stuffing legs and arms. Heavy-weight interfacing is ideal for pattern making if you think you will be making several dolls from the same design and wish to store your patterns for re-use.

PRETTY EFFECTS

Trimmings all help to finish a doll's appearance and to create the character.

The notions counters of large stores have good ranges for you to choose from but narrow or small scale trims can sometimes be difficult to find. Ribbons are available from a tiny 1/16in (1.5mm) wide up to 3in (7.5cm) wide, and the colour range is extensive. Narrow lace edgings can often be found and eyelet insertion from 1/8-1/4in (3-6mm) wide is available. Braids are useful for skirt hems and help to give felt garments a good finish. Some braids, around 1/2in (12mm) wide can be cut through the middle to make narrow braids.

Artificial flowers should be in your collection of trimmings. Buy very cheap sprays and break them down into individual flowers.

Start a collection of tiny buttons, beads and sequins so that you have a choice when you need it for your dolls. However, anything decorative which can be tugged off should be avoided when making dolls for young children. They won't notice that

FABRICS FOR DOLL-MAKING

Bodies Pale pink, cream or natural-coloured fabrics for caucasian dolls. Brown and beige for oriental or African dolls. White stockinette or pure cotton fabrics can be soaked in cold tea to give them a light tint. Felt can be used for bodies but cannot be washed. Cotton, cotton poplin, calico, flannelette, stockinette, poly/cotton.

Dresses, blouses, skirts
All of the above fabrics plus silk, rayon, thin wool, wool/polyester mixes, voile, spotted swiss, broderie anglaise, lawn, batiste, ginghams, Madras cotton, nun's veiling, organza.

Trousers, shorts, dungarees
Cotton, cotton/polyester mixes, medium-weight wool, denim, fine needlecord.

Underwear and blouses
Cambric, lawn, fine polyester/cotton mixes, dotted Swiss, broderie anglaise, cotton jersey, stockinette.

PATTERN MAKING MATERIALS
The patterns in this book are given in two forms, direct trace-offs and as diagrams. You may sometimes meet another form of pattern – the graph pattern.

Some equipment will be required to prepare patterns for doll making.

Direct trace-off patterns
To use these, you will need sheets of tracing paper or kitchen greaseproof paper. The tracing paper is laid over the book page and taped down at the edges with small pieces of Sellotape or Scotchtape. Trace the image with a sharply-pointed HB pencil.

Very simple shapes, such as squares or circles, may be drawn directly on to the wrong side of smooth fabrics, using either a soft pencil or dressmaker's chalk pencil. If fabrics are very thin and transparent, full-sized patterns can be direct-traced from the page, using a finely sharpened HB pencil, or an coloured embroidery pencil. Another useful marking device is a pen which has air-soluble ink in it. After tracing a pattern the line remains on the fabric for a short time, and usually after sewing, it has disappeared.

the trimmings aren't there and will love your creation just the same.

STUFFINGS AND FILLINGS
Most dolls are stuffed somewhere in the body or head and filling is one of the most important techniques in doll making. A poor, lumpy filling can spoil even the most exquisitely made doll. There are different kinds available – foam chips, polystyrene granules, cut-up waste fabric, kapok etc among them. None of these is recommended. Polyester fibre toy filling, which is flameproof, has been used for the toys in this book, as it conforms to health and safety standards. It washes well, dries quickly, is lightweight and is very resilient. Polyester filling has the added advantage that it is white so it is ideal for stuffing dolls with pale fabric heads and bodies.

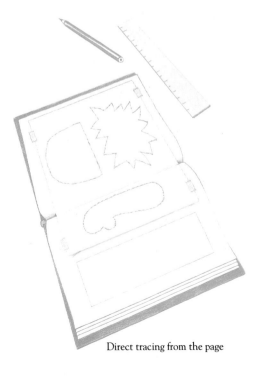

Direct tracing from the page

Diagram patterns

It is recommended that these are copied on to squared graph paper, using a ruler and a sharply-pointed HB pencil.

The lines on the paper will help you to keep corners square and accurate. You may find a flexible plastic ruler (obtainable from art shops and suppliers) an aid when drawing curves. The ruler can be easily bent into a curve and then you simply pencil along its edge. The pattern shapes can either be cut directly from the graph paper or, if you wish to keep the pattern for repeated use, trace it on to tracing paper.

Graph patterns

These patterns are given reduced in size on a squared grid. A scale is given and, to produce a full-sized pattern, you need squared dressmaker's paper marked with squares of the same scale. This paper is sold in large sheets, several to a packet, and can be obtained from dressmaking notions counters in shops and department stores.

To reproduce a graph pattern you copy the lines on your pattern paper, square for square. Graph patterns are not given for any of the projects in this book.

Transferring patterns

Patterns are transferred to the fabric with dressmaker's carbon paper. This is sold in sheets in packets of three or four colours, red, blue, yellow and white. A sheet is slipped between the pattern and fabric, and then the lines traced over with a tracing tool or a sharply-pointed HB pencil.

MAKING A START

Before attempting to use a pattern, it is important that you study the information given on it. This will take the form of words, numerals, letters, arrows and other symbols and is provided so that you cut out the correct number of pieces, arrange the fabric with the grain in the right direction and cut along folded fabric or from doubled fabric when required. Patterns also have 'balance marks' on them. These are set at the edge of the patterns and assist you in matching pattern pieces correctly. The information provided is essential to the success of the project.

Preparing patterns

Trace full-sized patterns (or drawn-out diagram patterns) on tracing or greaseproof paper spacing pieces about an inch (2.5cm) apart. When a pattern piece is large, it may be split on the page and arrows will indicate where the two pieces are to be joined. Trace the largest piece, move the tracing paper and trace the remaining section.

Some pattern pieces are shown as one half only (the Two-faced dolls pattern, for instance). To make a complete pattern, lay the folded edge of your tracing paper against the fold line on the master pattern (this will usually be marked 'place to fold'). Trace the outline, unfold the paper, refold and then trace again. If two toys have a shared outline (such as the Prince and the Frog upside-down doll), trace the shared outlines separately for each doll, then add

Enlarging a graph pattern

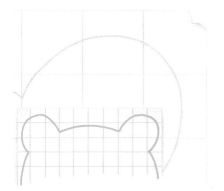

Left: Lay folded tracing on the half master pattern, trace and open the tracing for the full pattern

Below: Brush your hand over fur or pile fabric to determine the direction of the pile

the relevant parts to complete the patterns.

Where patterns instruct that you cut more than one piece from the fabric, cut from doubled fabric. If you are working from a fabric which is not sold ready-folded (such as felt), then cut the pattern piece out once, then reverse the pattern and cut out again.

The instructions always remind you to 'put in all marks, words and letters' on your pattern. Make sure that you do this. On most patterns, you will see an arrow indicated. This is to indicate 'straight grain' on evenly woven fabrics or 'direction of pile' on velvet or fur fabrics. Pin the pattern so that the arrow lies along the weft (or warp) on woven fabric or along the pile on pile fabrics. (Brush the pile with your hand and the direction in which you smooth is the direction in which the arrow should point.)

When pinning patterns to fur fabric, make sure the directional arrow follows the pile

Seam allowances

Always read through the pattern instructions to check whether the pattern includes a seam allowance or if one is to be added when cutting out. For toys, the pattern allowance is usually 3/8in (9mm or 1cm). Most of the patterns in this book tell you to add the seam allowance when cutting out.

Pinning out

Spread the fabric on your working surface (if it has become badly creased, press to remove the creases). Cut out the paper pattern pieces and arrange them on the fabric, taking note of the straight grain or direction of pile arrows, and of any

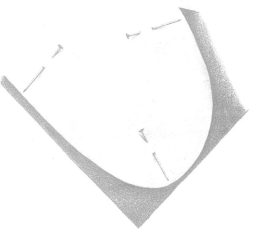

Set pins at right angles to the pattern edge

instructions to place pieces to the fold of the fabric. If seam allowance is included on the pattern, pieces can be positioned quite close together. If seam allowance is to be added, then arrange them at least 1in (2.5cm) apart. Pin the pattern to the fabric, setting pins at right angles to the pattern edge. Take up only a little fabric with the pin and have the pin head inside the edge of the pattern, so that it does not get in the way of the scissors when you are cutting out. Set pins about 2in (5cm) apart. If the seam allowance has been included, cut out round the pattern edge. If it to be added, cut out 3/8in (9mm or 1cm) away from the pattern.

Sewing tip

When instructions indicate that the seam allowance is to be added, first re-fold the fabric, right sides facing. Pin out the pattern. Draw round the outline of the pattern pieces using pencil or dressmaker's chalk pencil. (Add all marks etc.) Cut out 3/8in (9mm) from the pattern edge. Unpin the pattern. Baste the fabric pieces together, and stitch along the chalked line. This method enables you to achieve accurate stitching and perfect, straight seams.

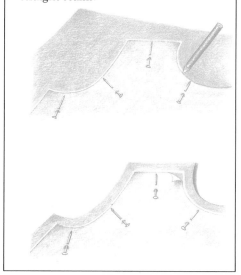

Marking the fabric

The marks on the pattern must now be transferred to the fabric. To do this, unpin the pattern along one side and slip a piece of dressmaker's carbon paper between the pattern and fabric and between the fabric layers. Re-pin and, using a sharpened HB pencil, mark in any fold lines, dots etc. Unpin the pattern. If the fabric is light-coloured, the carbon paper marks will be clearly seen on the fabric. If the fabric is patterned, you should transfer marks using tailor's tacks.

Tailor's tacks

These are worked before the pattern is unpinned. Thread a needle with basting thread and pull it doubled. Take a double stitch through the pattern and both thicknesses of fabric, on the spot to be marked, leaving a loop. Cut the thread end. When all the tailor's tacks have been worked, unpin the pattern and gently pull the fabric layers apart. Snip the threads between the layers. The place is thus marked with threads. This method of marking is also used on thick or rough-surfaced fabrics.

Never mark matching 'V's by clipping into the seam allowance - this weakens it. Cut the 'V' outwards from the pattern edge.

Snip the threads between the layers

Basting

Before stitching, the fabric pieces should first be pinned and then basted together. Matching marks, pin pieces together, right sides facing, following the pattern instruction. Thread a needle with basting thread and knot the end. Work medium-length running stitches just inside the stitching line, removing the pins as you go. Finish with a backstitch. (Remember to count your pins before pinning and afterwards, to make sure that none are left in your work.)

Pin and baste all pieces.

If the instructions tell you to pierce holes for eyes, or attach features to heads before joining pieces, do it now.

STITCHING AND SEWING

In the instructions, stitching means working on a sewing machine and sewing means working by hand. However, if you want to work your doll entirely by hand, use small running stitches or neat backstitching.

To machine-stitch, set the machine to a small-to-medium stitch and run the machine backwards and forwards for a stitch or two at the start of a seam and at the end. When hand sewing, begin and end with a backstitch.

Join all pieces in the order given in the pattern instructions. Press every seam as it is completed, then remove the basting threads.

Seams and finishes

In doll making, you will mostly be using an ordinary straight seam, where two pieces of fabric are pinned and basted together and stitching is worked along the seam line. Occasionally, for special dolls, French seams, which have a neat finish on the wrong side of work, are recommended for their clothes.

On curved edges and inverted corners, you will be asked to clip into the seam allowance. This is to ease the fabric and prevent the seam from puckering. If seams are too wide or thick, trimming the width back to 1/8in (3mm) will be recommended or you will be instructed to layer the seam allowance. This is sometimes important where a second line of stitching crosses a join - such as when sewing the inner leg seams of trousers or shorts.

Trim seam allowances with pinking shears to prevent fraying, or work oversewing along the seam edges. If you have a sewing machine with a zigzag stitch facility, set the stitch to a wide zigzag and work over the seam allowance edges.

Perfect curved seams

When sewing a curved seam, you will find that you get less drag and distortion on the seam if you start at the halfway point, and stitch each side separately.

BIAS BINDING

Bias binding is available in both cotton and rayon or polyester satin, and in a variety of widths. This is a useful finish in doll making and can be used to edge armholes and necklines and finish off hems. To apply binding, baste one raw edge to the garment raw edge, right sides facing. Machine-stitch, then turn the other raw edge to the inside and hem or slipstitch in place, thus enclosing the raw edge of the garment.

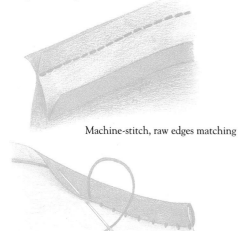

Machine-stitch, raw edges matching

Slipstitch the turned edge in place

Gather cuffs or necklines with ribbons or tapes through casings

along the bottom fold. Snip a hole in the casing in an unobtrusive place and oversew the edges. Thread ribbon or tape through the casing using a bodkin. If the doll is for a child, pull up the casing to the desired length, then catch the ribbon or tape in place, so that it cannot be pulled from the casing.

FASTENINGS

Press fasteners are mostly recommended in this book because they are easier for children to cope with and buttonholes tend to wear out. Where buttons have been used, they are sewn to the front of the opening as a decoration. Hooks and eyes are considered rather fiddly and zip fasteners are generally too large scale for dolls. Ribbon or fabric ties are ideal for doll's clothes. To attach these, fold over one end and sew to the garment with tiny hemming stitches. Cut the other end of ribbon ties in a fishtail. Neaten the end of a fabric tie by turning and sewing a neat hem.

Ribbons or tapes through stitched casing are a pretty way of gathering necklines, cuffs and waists. To make a casing on an edge, turn and press a narrow hem, then turn the hem again to the desired depth. Machine-stitch along the top fold and then

---

Sewing with felt

Cut felt shapes out in the same way as woven fabric, pinning the pattern to it. Marking is best done with tailor tacks. When cutting out small shapes, either iron the felt on to interfacing, to stiffen the edges, or press the felt on to a small self-adhesive label. This helps you to cut out with a firm edge. Remove the paper afterwards.

Felt can be machine-stitched or hand-sewn with running stitches. Use machine zigzag stitches for neatening and finishing cut edges. Necklines and armholes on doll's clothes made of felt can be bound with bias binding, or finished with buttonhole or blanket stitches.

EMBROIDERY STITCHES

There are literally hundreds of embroidery stitches to choose from when you are decorating fabric but only a few are used in this book.

Satin stitch

This is used for filling shapes (such as eyes). Work stitches evenly and so that they touch. Bring the needle through at A, insert it at B and bring it through again at C.

Straight stitch

In doll making, straight stitches are often used for indicating eyelashes and sometimes for attaching felt eyes. The stitches are worked in an eight-point star. Bring the needle through at A, insert it at B and bring it through again at C.

Back stitch

This stitch, properly worked, looks like machine-stitching and can be used for seaming. Bring the needle through at A, insert it at B and bring it out at C in front of A.

Stem stitch

This is often recommended for outlining eyes, and for indicating eyebrows and mouths. Bring the needle through at A, the thread below the needle. Insert it at B and bring it through again at C.

Chain stitch

This decorative stitch is sometimes used for outlining eyes and noses. Bring the needle through at A and, with the thread below the needle, insert it beside A at B, The thread forms a loop. Bring the needle through at C, pull through gently, ready to start the next chain stitch. Detached chain stitch To work this stitch, from C, work a tying stitch over the loop.

French knot

Although French knots are a decorative stitch, in this book they are sometimes used to highlight eyes. Bring the needle through at A, wind the thread round the needle twice and then insert the point at B, close by A. Pull the thread through so that the knot tightens on the fabric surface.

SEWING STITCHES

Hand sewing is almost a forgotten art but working with a needle and thread on fine fabric is a most relaxing occupation. In doll making, a few hand sewing stitches are needed to achieve a good finish.

Running stitch

This stitch can be used to join pieces of fabric together if there is not going to be a strain on the seam. It is also used for gathering fabric. Begin with a small backstitch, pick up several small, even stitches on the needle and pull the needle through. If you are working a seam, work a backstitch occasionally to strengthen the seam.

Gathering

Running stitch is used for gathering fabric. Work as for running stitch and leave a length of thread at the end of the row for pulling up the gathers.

Oversewing

This simple stitch is useful for joining to edges of fabric together (particularly felt) and can also be used to neaten seam edges to prevent them from fraying. Working from right to left, bring the needle through at A and insert the needle from the back of the work at B, bringing it through to the front at C, ready to start the next stitch. Keep stitches small and evenly spaced.

Basting

This is used to hold two pieces of fabric together termporarily. Work it in the same way as running stitch but make the stitches longer, about 1/4in (6mm) long with a 1/4in (6mm) space between each stitch.

Hemming

Hemming is worked from right to left, taking up 2 threads of the fabric at the fold of the hem. Insert the needle obliquely on the edge of the fold.

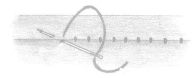

Slip stitch

When worked correctly, this stitch is almost invisible on the surface of the work. It is usually used for closing a seam. Work from right to left and bring the needle up through the folded edge of the fabric. Pick up a thread or two on the opposite fabric edge then slip the needle through the folded edge for about 1/8in (3mm). Bring the needle through and pull gently.

Ladder stitch

This is used for closing openings and also for attaching ears, limbs etc. It is simple a running stitch, the stitches taken first on one side of the opening, then on the other. As you work, turn seam allowances to the inside with the needle point.

STUFFING DOLLS

Stuffing dolls is an art and care should be taken at this most important stage. Use a good quality, washable polyester toy filling. Follow the pattern instructions for the correct order in which to stuff the toy. The secret is to tease the filling and then insert only small pieces at a time. The surface of the doll should be smooth and well-rounded. Roll and smooth the limbs to check that there are no lumpy places. Generally, heads, legs and arms are stuffed firmly, with less stuffing at the joints so that the doll is flexible. Use your fingers, a blunt pencil, scissors points or a specially made stuffing stick to push stuffing into small places. If you need to rearrange stuffing, push a long, thin darning needle through the fabric and move the tip around until the stuffing is redistributed to your liking.

Some dolls, such as those intended to stand up, require firm stuffing throughout. Others are softly stuffed so that they are cuddly. Some designs require a combination of both effects. The pattern instructions will tell you the degree of stuffing required for your doll.

After stuffing, close the open seam with slip stitches, prick stitch or with ladder stitch.

FACES AND FEATURES

The features are probably the most important part of doll making. Spend as much time as possible at this stage, because clumsy work can mar the doll's appearance - and a child can be completely averse to a doll whose face he thinks is unattractive or menacing. If eyes, for instance, are set too close together, or too high on the head, the doll can look bad temperered. Big black eyes, without highlight or other decoration, sometimes look staring and hypnotic. The pictures in this book will guide you in achieving the correct expression for the dolls but always plan the eyes, nose and mouth positions before glueing on pieces or starting embroidery. Mark them in with a sharpened embroidery chalk pencil - the marks will brush away afterwards.

Embroidered features are best for fabric dolls because they last and cannot be accidentally pulled off during play. Some of the dolls in this book have buttons or beads for eyes. This is acceptable if the doll is for decorative purposes but do not use this method if the doll is for a young child.

Eyes

If eyes are being embroidered directly on to a doll's face. it is often easier to do this before stuffing the head, when you can still get your hand inside. However, work after stuffing, if you find this suits you better. There are various ways of working eyes, depending on the character of the dolls and the expression you want to achieve.

Embroidered eyes Work the entire eye in satin stitch, using 2 strands of stranded embroidery cotton in the needle. Work the eyeball in white or cream, the iris in blue or brown and the pupil in black. Make sure that the stitches are even and touching, so that a smooth surface is achieved. A highlight can be added to the pupil with a white French knot. If you like, work straight stitch eyelashes radiating from the upper eyelid afterwards.

Felt eyes Felt is the most popular material for eyes and all kinds of expressions can be achieved quite easily. Some examples are shown on page 110.

For a basic felt eye, cut a circle of white felt, then another of darker coloured felt, but a little smaller. Glue the dark circle to the light, then when it is dry, hem all round the edges to secure the dark circle in position. Sew the assembled eye to the doll's face.

The darker circle can be placed to the left or to the right of the white circle to give the effect of the doll looking sideways. Always make sure that both eyes are looking in the same direction when you sew them on.

Pie-slice eyes These look effective on rag dolls. Cut 2 white circles and 2 black, of the same size. Cut a 'slice' from the black circles. Glue, then stitch the black circles on the white, making sure that the 'slice' is at the same angle on both eyes. Sew the eyes to the doll's face.

Eyes Ideas

1. Eye embroidered in satin stitch.

2 Straight stitches over a felt circle.

3. Felt circle with chain stitch outline.

4. Pie slice eye in felt.

5. Felt circle and straight stitch eyelashes.

6. Button and stem stitch eyelashes.

7. Straight stitches in a cross.

Noses

On most dolls, the nose is just a few stitches in Stem stitch. If a more pronounced nose is required, cut a circle of the face fabric and gather up the edges. Stuff with a little toy filling, then sew the nose to the doll's face with ladder stitches.

Mouths

If these are to be embroidered, work them in stem stitch or chain stitch using 2 strands of stranded embroidery cotton. Use pale pinks for girl dolls, working the lower lip in a darker shade. Use brown for boy dolls. Red thread can be used but you may find it looks a little hard, except on the faces of character dolls. Remember that a curved line for a mouth will give a doll a happier expression.

Hair styles

There are many different yarns and fabrics that can be used to make doll's hair. Knitting wool is used mostly in this book but you can also use stranded embroidery cotton, soft cotton, frayed string, raffia and fabric strips. These materials can either be applied directly to the doll's head and then styled or you can make separate 'wigs' and then attach them to the doll.

Skein wigs These are the easiest and most popular way of making doll's hair styles. First, estimate how long the hair should be by measuring from the centre of the head to the desired length. Double this measurement and add 3in (7.5cm). Cut a piece of card to the desired length of hair and wind wool round it. Cut the loops at either end and sew across the skein, using backstitch, to hold the strands together. Place the skein on the doll's head and backstitch along the 'parting' into the crown.

The hair can be styled in different ways - tying it in bunches on either side of the face, plaiting, tying at the back of the head with a ribbon bow. For a variation, add a fringe by making a short skein and sewing this across the crown, just above the hairline, then sew the main skein wig over the top.

For a ponytail or chignon, you need long lengths of wool. Measure round the doll's head and cut the card to this measurement and to the depth required. Wind the wool round and sew across the skein as before. The skein should be long enough to encircle the doll's head. Place the wig on the doll and sew round the forehead, along the same line of stitching. Pull all the wool back towards the crown of the head and arrange in the style required.

Curly hair Wind wool around narrow strips of stiff paper. Sew along the centre then tear the paper away either side of the stitching. Sew the curls to the doll's head, starting on the crown and sewing spirally round until the head is covered.

RIBBONS, LACE AND BOWS
Ribbons and lace make pretty finishing touches to rag dolls' clothes and should always be sewn in place very securely.

Edgings and bands
Baste the ribbon or lace in position, before making up the garment. Machine-stitch along both edges.

For a neat finish on hem, baste ribbon, press the turning to the right side, then baste and stitch the ribbon to the right side, covering the raw edge. This ensures that no raw edges show on the wrong side of the garment.

Tassels Cut a long length of very narrow ribbon (or stranded embroidery thread). Fold the length until the bunch is about 3in (7.5cm) long. Tie a knot in the middle. Bring the side loops down and then bind round the bunch, just under the knot, using matching thread. Tie the threads ends tightly. Snip the folded ends to make the tassel.

Knot the bunch, then bind round just under the knot

Bows
Although ribbon bows can be tied and then sewn in place, you will find the following method makes a better bow. Cut a piece of ribbon and form into a ring, the ends overlapping. Gather the middle, sewing through all thicknesses. Cut a small piece of ribbon, fold around the middle of the bow tightly and sew to secure it at the back. To give the bow tails, cut a piece of ribbon and 'fishtail' the ends. Gather the middle and sew behind the bow.

Hair Styles

Skein wig stiched in place

The main wig stiched over the fringe

Tied in bunches at the side

Try plaiting the side strands

The fringe stitched across the head

Cut ends short for a boy doll

Acknowledgment

The author thanks Valerie Webb and
Hercules, her cat, for the loan of the
doorstop cat on page 58.